Presented to

By

On the Occasion of

Date

© 2002 by Barbour Publishing, Inc.

Cover design © PhotoDisc, Inc.

ISBN 1-58660-393-0

Published by Barbour Books, an imprint of Barbour Publishing, Inc., P.O. Box 719, Uhrichsville, Ohio 44683
www.barbourbooks.com

Member of the
Evangelical Christian
Publishers Association

Printed in the United States of America.

ALONE WITH GOD

Biblical Inspiration for the Unmarried

MICHAEL WARDEN

BARBOUR BOOKS

An Imprint of Barbour Publishing, Inc.

I would like
you to be free from concern.
An unmarried man is concerned
about the Lord's affairs—
how he can please the Lord. . . .
An unmarried woman or virgin
is concerned about the Lord's affairs:
Her aim is to be devoted to
the Lord in both body and spirit.

1 Corinthians 7:32, 34

INTRODUCTION

STOP believing the lie that tells you that you are single only because you "have issues" with men or women. You are not single because you are broken, or because you are unacceptable in some way. The very idea is ludicrous! We are all broken vessels—whether married, divorced, or single. It is good to recognize your brokenness, but never curse yourself because you are a broken vessel. That is exactly the sort of vessel that God delights in using.

You are single because you are chosen by God to walk in single-minded devotion to Him. Singleness is a calling as surely as marriage or parenthood, and one calling is not greater than another. You may be called to singleness for a year, a decade, or a lifetime. However long you are called to be single, do not waste this opportunity to do something extraordinary for God.

The advantage of being single is that you can be single-minded for God in a way that married folk cannot. And that is a very powerful advantage for anyone who seeks abundant life in Christ. But today's church has done a great disservice to singles when it promotes married life above the single life as a "more mature" Christian way of life. Nothing in Scripture supports that claim. Yet, strangely, many church folk make that claim—either in their speech or in their attitude. Don't let popular opinion dissuade you from embracing the opportunity God has given you. Instead, make up your mind to see the single life for what it is—one of the most intimate gifts God can give.

DAY 1

Jesus answered,
"The work of God is this:
to believe in the one he has sent."
JOHN 6:29

WE are always trying to add something to Jesus' equation for following God. We are not comfortable simply believing like children; we'd rather believe a little, then finish up the task with our own efforts.

But the work of God is literally "God's work." By definition, it is a supernatural work and cannot benefit in the slightest from your efforts to "make it happen." All that is required of you is your absolute, continual surrender, and a faith that compels you to keep your heart focused on Jesus.

"Do you mean I must simply sit in my room and pray, and wait for my food to be cooked, and my bills to be paid?" No, but you must learn to walk as Jesus did. You are in Christ as Christ is in the Father. Jesus is the hand; you are the glove. The glove can do nothing by itself; it can only do what the hand is doing.

To believe in Jesus means to abide in Him, and to allow His life to be manifest through you. That is the work of God. It is not about you or your ideas or your plans or your efforts. It's about Jesus. To accomplish God's work, you must follow Jesus—and Jesus alone.

*"If you then,
being evil, know how
to give good gifts to your children,
how much more shall your heavenly Father
give the Holy Spirit to those who ask Him?"*

LUKE 11:13 NAS

GOD the Father has made provision for you every day. Knowing this, it seems odd that we so often demand that God continually lay His provision out in plain sight before we will really trust in it. "Oh, I know God will provide for my need," we say. "I'd just feel so much better if I could see some sign of His provision." But once we rest in the truth that God provides for us, we no longer need to see proof to believe it is true. It simply is. Unshakeable. Fact. We will find a great deal of rest in that sort of faith.

Do not get in the habit of trusting in what you can see. What you see circumstantially can be deceiving. All such things are passing—a moment here, the next moment gone. But God's Word is not deceptive. It is always true, unchanging, and can always be trusted. Does God love you? Yes. Does God command the storehouses of heaven? Yes. Then will He not use all that is at His disposal to care for you? Of course. So relax.

When you are hungering in need, do not think

that God has abandoned you. He never will. God's desire for you, and His command, is that you rest and believe. Let your Father care for you in the way He has chosen. His way is best, regardless of what your intellect tells you.

DAY 3

*"And he humbled
you and let you be hungry,
and fed you with manna which you
did not know, nor did your fathers know, that
He might make you understand that man
does not live by bread alone, but man
lives by everything that proceeds
out of the mouth of the LORD."*
DEUTERONOMY 8:3 NAS

GOD'S providence allows you to be in need. He does not do this to punish or forsake your heart, but rather to refine you. He longs to make your heart pure. He knows there are things in you that will rise up to doubt Him when difficulties come. So come they do, that He may reveal the darkness in you, and provoke you to bring it into the light.

What do you hunger for? The hunger you face is for your testing, nothing more. You need not doubt that He will meet the need. He will. But first He will see what is in your heart. He knows there is still darkness in you and uses your need as a refining fire that separates the impurities from your soul.

Jesus loves you more than life itself. His heart never wants to hurt you or leave you in need forever. But these things must happen for you to be free. More than anything, Jesus is determined that you be free. Believe in Him, whatever your need. Work with Him, and do not doubt. Then, together, you will remake your heart.

DAY 4

"They [Israel] turned their backs to me and not their faces; though I taught them again and again, they would not listen or respond to discipline. They set up their abominable idols in the house that bears my Name and defiled it."

JEREMIAH 32:33–34

IT is possible to lose the Promised Land once it is gained, but in only one way—through idolatry. Idolatry is worshipping anything other than God. Such idols take many seductive forms—family, career, entertainment, comfort, money, pleasure, education, and even religion. Pride itself is a very common form of idolatry—the worship of self.

The Promised Land is gained through battle, and it is kept through diligence and humility. That is why the Scripture rightly says, "Watch over your heart with all diligence, for from it flow the springs of life" (Proverbs 4:23 NAS). The springs of abundant life are not in the external world. They are within you. And they can be stolen if they are not guarded. But how do you guard your heart? By staying humble in everything. Humble toward God, and humble toward others. In every circumstance, humility is your truest defense against the idols that want to steal our heart away.

Idolatry is an issue of the heart long before it becomes a matter of behavior. You can look perfectly holy on the outside and still embrace an abominable idol in your soul. Therefore, be diligent to guard your heart. Pursue humility in all things. This is your best defense. Fight for what is yours in the Lord. And stand guard over what you have gained.

*But we are not of those
who shrink back to destruction,
but of those who have faith to the preserving
of the soul. Now faith is the assurance of things
hoped for, the conviction of things not seen.*

HEBREWS 10:39–11:1 NAS

YOU are made of better stuff than you think. So when the trial arises, you generally give up far too easily. One small sting hits your heart, and you throw up your arms in despair, ready to give up. But God knows the stuff you are made of. He knows your limits, and your capacity for faith. And so He allows the sting to come.

We will gain the daily strength we need in one way only—by looking to God as a child looks to a father. We will gain great confidence from God's face. "Those who look to him are radiant; their faces are never covered with shame" (Psalm 34:5).

Then the trials inevitably come. In the struggle, our childlike focus is diverted from God, and we allow circumstance to direct our lives. But circumstance is mindless—it cannot direct you to life, only to survival. Keep your focus on Jesus. He is your true shepherd. Listen to His Word, watch His movements. Stay close to Him, as little children do.

When the sting comes, persevere and don't waver

in faith. Don't look down. Rather, look at your hand held tight in Christ's, and look at the view from the heights where He has brought you. This, too, is His gift to you.

DAY 6

Beloved, now we
are children of God, and it has not appeared
as yet what we shall be. We know that,
when He appears, we shall be like Him,
because we shall see Him just as He is.
And everyone who has this hope fixed on
Him purifies himself, just as He is pure.
I JOHN 3:2–3 NAS

WE are not changed by the strength of our will or the depth of our desire. We are changed by seeing God—the one true reality. God is real. His love for you is real. His Word is real. Your relationships with other believers are real. But almost nothing else is. The rest is temporary illusion. See that house or that mountain? In time it will disappear as though it never existed. One of the great definitions of reality is this: that which is permanent and eternal.

When you begin to look to God as the one true reality, something wondrous happens. Your eyes are opened to see, and your ears are opened to hear. For the first time, you begin to see God (who is and defines reality), and you are changed. You cannot sit in the presence of God and not be changed. You begin to transform your mind and understand that you are not a shadow. You are real—an eternal being living in a temporary reality.

Once you begin to see God as the one true reality, all the things around you that are not real suddenly become obvious. You see that it does no good at all to put your hope in money, or possessions, or marriage, or the strength of your own soul. All of those things are illusions—shadows that do not exist in the eternal reality of God's presence. Instead, you must fix your eyes on Jesus and hope boldly in Him.

DAY 7

"Can a woman forget her nursing child,
and have no compassion on the son of her womb?
Even these may forget, but I will not forget you.
Behold, I have inscribed you on the palms of My
hands; your walls are continually before Me."
ISAIAH 49:15–16 NAS

THERE is a sense of "home" in all of us. It is that hard-to-define ache that continually tells you that there is something more for you somewhere, that you have not yet arrived at your goal. I'm not talking about the longing for heaven, but rather the longing for fulfillment on earth, the longing for a place to belong, to love and be loved, to be free here, in this world. This longing is hard-wired into our souls. It's part of being human.

God knows all about your longing, of course. He knows more about it than you ever will. And He is guiding you to your desired haven. You are not forsaken; He cannot forget you. Together, you are always moving toward the land of your inheritance. Step by step, you are occupying the kingdom.

But here is the part where you may get confused. You may think this longing is solely for something "out there," something circumstantial. A new career, a spouse, a family, an array of pricey possessions. Perhaps you get lost looking for outward changes and forget that the kingdom of God must first transform you—in the secret places of your soul—before any outward change will satisfy. Once the kingdom is established within you, then it will spill over into the external world around you.

*When Peter saw
him, he asked, "Lord,
what about him?" Jesus answered,
"If I want him to remain alive until I return,
what is that to you? You must follow me."*

JOHN 21:21–22

EACH of us has a path set before us by God. The paths are as varied as the people the Lord made them for, but they all lead to Christ. Your path is before you now, though you may not see it clearly. Don't worry; each step will be made clear by the Word of God and His Spirit within you. Like all paths in Christ, yours is a path of richness and intimacy and good fruit.

But it isn't the only path before you. There are others laid before you every day, paths created from your own desires or from the desires of others. God has allowed life to be this way, to give you the free will to choose the path you wish. If you do not choose God's path by a conscious act of your will, then you will choose death by default.

Beware of choosing the path that goes along with the crowd—even if the crowd is full of Christians. Only Christ knows the specific path He has called you to follow. The true path of God for you is the way of His Word and of His Spirit living within you. Follow that path faithfully, every moment, and do not try to make it look like everyone else's. Be true to Christ's way in you.

DAY 9

Therefore, since we are surrounded by such a great cloud of witnesses, let us throw off everything that hinders and the sin that so easily entangles, and let us run with perseverance the race marked out for us.
HEBREWS 12:1

THIS is a sobering command. It is the Lord's will for you to give yourself exclusively to one purpose—to shake loose any obstacles that hinder your way in God and run freely with abandon down the path He has chosen for you. Such freedom requires a long, steady obedience in the same direction. It is not just a neat idea. It is not just a philosophy. It is God's will for your life.

To live this way narrows your daily options. From the rising of the sun until it sets, your awareness of the world around you, your intelligence, your responsibilities, your daily tasks—all of these are to be continually submitted to God. When you do this, you will find that your life becomes wonderfully simple. "I desire, Lord, to do Your will"—nothing more, nothing less. And His response to your prayer becomes your only motivation in the natural realm. In this abandoned place of intimacy, He becomes the beginning and the end of everything you do. He truly becomes your all in all.

*What is more,
I consider everything a loss
compared to the surpassing greatness
of knowing Christ Jesus my Lord,
for whose sake I have lost all things.
I consider them rubbish, that I may gain Christ.*
PHILIPPIANS 3:8

WHEN you obey God's will to this degree, you find you can no longer say, "Oh, I will take up the cause again tomorrow. For now, I will give in to my old ways." The old ways are dead. You are committed now.

To reach such a place of abandoned freedom may take two years of consistent obedience to His will for your life. It may take one year, or five, or twenty. But such a harvest as you are looking for cannot be rushed. Do you dare to obey the Lord God to such an extreme degree? If you do, then take these truths to heart. They will strengthen you to finish the course:

- Recognize that you are living as an alien in a foreign land. This is not your home.
- Meditate daily on truths regarding your true identity in Christ.
- Practice living consciously in God's presence.
- Bring every thought captive to the obedience of Christ.
- Surround yourself with people who bear the Christlike qualities you wish to gain.
- Recognize that freedom is a process of sowing and reaping. Be patient and enjoy the journey!

DAY 11

But He, having offered one sacrifice for sins for all time, sat down at the right hand of God, waiting from that time onward until His enemies be made a footstool for His feet.
HEBREWS 10:12–13 NAS

LIKE Jesus, you also must at times wait on God to do what He has promised. God places a promise into your spirit—a promise that He confirms through His Word and through other believers—and you act in obedience to it. But nothing happens immediately. And so you wait, hoping God will someday bring the fulfillment of what He has promised to you. But

God never intended that we wait in hope, but rather that we wait in faith.

Hope can only say, "I hope this happens" or "I am praying for this to happen." But if God has really spoken to you, and you are confident of His voice, then you must do more than hope. You must believe. "Faith is the assurance of things hoped for" (Hebrews 11:1 NAS). Faith says, "I know this will happen; I am confident in God." Faith knows that the fulfillment of the promise God has spoken has come already—it's just a matter of time for it to come to present reality.

Waiting purifies your faith. So commit yourself to waiting patiently. Don't become discouraged when you round a bend and don't see your fulfillment right away. It will come. He makes everything beautiful in its time (Ecclesiastes 3:11). For now, enjoy the journey. Revel in the moment and let the waiting stretch your faith. Enjoy the gifts God has already brought today, and walk in faith for tomorrow.

DAY 12

Let us fix our eyes on Jesus,
the author and perfecter of our faith. . .
so that you will not grow weary and lose heart.
HEBREWS 12:2, 3

IT'S easy to forget and live only in the everyday mundane world. Life becomes merely functional, a series of tasks and duties strung together without meaning. You survive, but you are not really alive. True living is a choice, and you must make it every day, each passing moment. It is not an easy thing to do—merely surviving is far easier—but you were made for greater things.

True living requires great discipline and focus. It takes a heart committed to live deliberately, to defend itself fiercely against unimportant distractions.

If "surviving" is analogous to clinging to the rocky ledge of a high and dangerous cliff, then true living means we must daringly let go and fall, purposefully choosing to place our safety and future in God's hands rather than trying to cling to life in our own strength. Letting go seems dangerous, but in the end, it is the only way that leads to any sort of real life at all.

Jesus is life. To truly live, you must "fix your eyes on Him"—His ability, His will, His love for you. It is a choice. And if you fail to make it deliberately each day, then you merely choose surviving by default.

Therefore, choose life—even if it seems to cost you everything. The fact is, it always will.

DAY 13

*For you have been born again,
not of perishable seed, but of imperishable,
through the living and enduring word of God.*

1 PETER 1:23

THE mind, the will, the emotions—the soul—is born of the world. Nothing that is born of this world is able to overcome the world. Only that which has been reborn—not of the flesh but of the Spirit through faith—can overcome the world.

There is only one way this rebirth happens in our lives—we receive God's Truth implanted (as a seed) through faith. Then we must nurture the truth by providing light and water. The light is the Bible, the authority by which all truth must be measured, tested, and proven. Meditating on the Word provides life—giving light to God's truth planted in our souls. The water is the Holy Spirit. Without the watering of the Spirit, any seed of truth within us will die. But wherever Truth and Spirit are brought together, new life—overcoming life—is born.

The process of the Word is a discipline of the

Christian life. It may not always be a pleasant process, but those trained by it will reap an abundance of peace and righteousness. Plant God's truth deep in your soul, and then nurture it faithfully. Lay aside your flesh, and rely on God's Spirit to accomplish whatever concerns you. Then wait patiently for the Word to be reborn in your heart. Only in this way will you overcome the world.

DAY 14

Let the one who has my word
speak it faithfully. . . .
"Is not my word like fire," declares the LORD,
"and like a hammer that breaks a rock in pieces?"
JEREMIAH 23:28, 29

GOD'S Word is powerful. And He has planted His Word deep within you—it will not fail. Because God knows His truth is within you, His glory rejoices over you. The Word that shines forth through you is greater than the glory of kings or queens. You are His trueborn child. You need not worry. . .about anything.

Don't become discouraged or let your heart become weighted with doubts or the pressures of the day. Know that the life of God within you will spring forth today—His Word is sure.

Stand faithful in joy. You are running a course with God that will not fail. True life has come, and it will have its way in you. So be confident. Victory doesn't depend on your ability. Your fulfillment rests fully on the sureness of God's Word—and His Word cannot fail.

"You will go out in joy and be led forth in peace; the mountains and hills will burst into song before you, and all the trees of the field will clap their hands" (Isaiah 55:12). Rise up in the grace God has provided for you today. Stand on the sureness of His Word in your heart.

DAY 15

Therefore, rid yourselves
of all malice and all deceit,
hypocrisy, envy, and slander of every kind.
Like newborn babies, crave pure spiritual milk,
so that by it you may grow up in your salvation.
1 PETER 2:1–2

LISTEN to the Word every day. As much as possible, do not focus on external things but on the transformation of your heart. Do the outward things as it seems good to you, but you must not neglect the true process of the Word. By it you are truly transformed to freedom. By the Word you live. Listen to the Word!

To listen well, you must clear your life of sinful distractions. Clogging your soul with subtle sins—feeling hateful toward another person, acting hypocritical or envious, or speaking ill of someone else—all of these (and many like them) choke your ability to take in the Word. Sanctification is a process of vigilance—not only over what comes into your life, but also over what comes out. Are you struggling to "connect" with God's Word? Do the verses seem hollow to you? Then consider your ways. It may be that subtle sins are hindering the process of the Word in your soul. A true follower of Christ doesn't examine his behaviors and choices and ask, "What's wrong with it?" A true follower examines every behavior and choice and asks, "What's right with it?" If something does not promote God's kingdom in your life or the lives of others, drop it. It's hardly worth your time. Rather, strive always to "redeem the time," and keep your soul sanctified and ready to receive God's Word every day.

*The LORD Almighty
has a day in store for all the proud
and lofty, for all that is exalted
(and they will be humbled).*

ISAIAH 2:12

FOR Christians, humility is a most powerful ally. Through humility, they receive grace (which is God's power for life). Through humility, they experience God's awesome presence. Humility provides a shield around them when they are attacked or maligned by others. The humble have nothing to hide, and no reason to feel shame. They know their weaknesses and offer them without reservation to God. And God, through their weaknesses, reveals His strength.

Are there things you consistently hide from others? Are there secrets about you that have you locked in shame? If so, then in those areas you are still struggling with pride. You do not want to be exposed. You do not want others to see your weakness. But you do not realize that hiding your weakness only deepens its hold on your soul. Humble yourself before God in that area of weakness. Invite Him to give you the grace to accept yourself in your brokenness—and to understand this redeeming truth: God takes broken things and makes them beautiful. His strength is perfected in our weakness.

If you remain in your shame, you will never know the fullness of joy in Christ. And you will certainly face a day of reckoning—when your pride will be exposed, and you will be humbled. Don't wait. Let humility become your strong ally in Christ.

DAY 17

Those who belong to Christ Jesus have crucified the sinful nature with its passions and desires.
GALATIANS 5:24

WHAT does your flesh really crave? Admiration? Comfort? Power? It's important to know the answer to that question so that you'll know, in a practical sense, what you're up against on a daily basis.

Too often, we Christians make deals with our flesh. We don't kill the sinful nature but keep it alive, locked in a cage perhaps, to serve as our escape when life gets hard. We are rejected, so we wallow in self-pity. We are weary of doing good unnoticed, so we praise ourselves under the guise of "sharing" our deeds with others. We are lonely, so we give in to sexual temptation to cover our pain. We face the trial of faith, and because it hurts, we stop believing.

There can be no compromise with the flesh. As

long as your flesh is given any place in your life, it will rule you from that place. Indulging your sinful nature can never bring you life, no matter how good it feels in the moment. It can only steal your freedom. You must kill these old reactions—daily if necessary—as they arise to challenge your walk to freedom. "So I say, live by the Spirit, and you will not gratify the desires of the sinful nature" (Galatians 5:16). The way to kill the flesh is to starve it. Ignore it, focusing wholly on the life of the Spirit within.

DAY 18

When I want to do good,
evil is right there with me.
ROMANS 7:21

I intend to love my sister in Christ, but I end up hurting her instead. I intend to do good to others, but end up doing good to myself and letting those "others" take care of themselves. It seems like I am plagued by a saboteur. A secret companion with a bag full of wrenches—just itching to throw them into every one of my well-intentioned plans. I want to do good, but there's evil right there with me.

The first step to overcoming any enemy is to recognize that he is there, and that he means you harm.

It's simply naïve to believe that your motives are always pure, that you generally aren't prone to selfishness, and that others are offended by you only because they are too sensitive or immature—not because of anything you've done. You may have intended to do good—and that is to your credit. But evil is right there with you. We would all be wise never to forget that.

Remember that your flesh is fallen. Don't try to win the war against your dark side with your own wits. Rather, stay humble, and fix your eyes on Jesus alone. Acknowledge Him in everything, and He will direct your steps toward genuine purity in everything you do. "But I say, walk by the Spirit, and you will not carry out the desire of the flesh" (Galatians 5:16 NAS).

DAY 19

Jesus gave them this answer:
"I tell you the truth,
the Son can do nothing by himself;
he can do only what he sees his Father doing, because
whatever the Father does the Son also does. For the
Father loves the Son and shows him all he does."
JOHN 5:19–20

CONSIDER this rewording of John 5:19–20:
"I tell you the truth, you can do nothing by your own

effort, unless it is something you see Jesus doing. For whatever Jesus does, these things you also should do in like manner. For Jesus loves you, and shows you all things that He Himself is doing."

You might say, "How can I live like this? I can't see Jesus out walking around like an ordinary man!" But "we walk by faith, not by sight" (2 Corinthians 5:7). God has given you the eyes of faith you need to "see" what Jesus is doing.

"But how will I know it's really God I'm seeing?" He has provided tools you can use to discern truth from error. Test the Spirit against the Word. When the Spirit is genuine, you will find that He always points to Christ.

If, however, you try to test the Spirit against your reasoning, and the reasoning of others around you, you will find nothing but confusion. Christians who trust their reason more than God's Spirit are like children fumbling around in a perfectly well-lit room—because they have closed the eyes of their faith and cannot see where they are going.

But you must not live this way. Dare to fix your eyes on Jesus. Believe (like a child) in the miracle that the living Christ is actually present with you. And begin to do whatever you see Him doing.

DAY 20

Jesus replied,
"You do not realize now what I am doing,
but later you will understand."
JOHN 13:7

WISDOM and learning come not from experience, but from our reactions to it. Learning from experience is a matter of choice. The nature of the experience is irrelevant; it is the attitude of the heart that determines what we get out of it. The lessons from experience are learned slowly, over time, like a seed planted in the ground. But when the plant finally bears fruit—when we finally understand—we are permanently changed.

Not everyone who goes through an experience will respond well, however. Some will simply forget about it—their seed is stolen away. Some will interpret the experience wrongly, or fail to apply the lesson to their lives—their seed is choked out by other concerns. But some will receive the lesson implanted, and they will be changed. Learning to be teachable in the midst of any experience—whether pleasant or painful—is the heart of wisdom.

Jesus uses experience to sift our hearts and separate out for Himself those whose hearts are teachable and willing. Experience beautifies the hearts of those who are humble and hardens the hearts of those who demand their own way. It's a decision of the heart. Do not resist Him, but commit yourself to remain moldable in His hand.

DAY 21

*"Let the little children come to me,
and do not hinder them,
for the kingdom of God belongs to such as these."*

MARK 10:14

CHILDREN know how to trust with abandon and joy. Think of a child's typical day. She rises with the sun and thinks of all the things she can do to enjoy the day. She does not worry about what she will eat or whether she will have clothes to wear. She has a home and does not even wonder if it might be taken away. Everything that belongs to her parents is hers, as well. She trusts her parents implicitly and without hesitation. She can imagine life in no other way.

Any Christian who is able to come to Jesus in this way will experience an abundance of love, joy, and peace every day. But most of us have been hurt by life, and now we come to Jesus as adults who are committed to providing for ourselves and protecting ourselves. To know the abundant life Jesus offers, you must let go of your control. You must stop protecting yourself.

(Christ is your defense.) You must stop taking responsibility to provide for yourself. (God is your provider.) The path back to innocence and trust is tricky, but it begins when you take the frightening step of allowing God to provide for you what you need.

With consistent obedience to the Word and the Spirit, leaning not on your own understanding, you will rediscover the amazing joy of being absolutely free from concern—the glorious freedom of the children of God.

DAY 22

If anyone competes as an athlete,
he does not win the prize
unless he competes according to the rules. . . .
Consider what I say, for the Lord will
give you understanding in everything.
2 TIMOTHY 2:5, 7 NAS

OUR private time with God is the most important and vital time of our day. It is the core around which everything else revolves. Yet too often we treat it like the least important time. We serve many things before we serve God and take our delight not in the joy of our relationship with God but in the sense of accomplishment we feel for having completed our daily "list" of necessary tasks.

Putting God first is not about time or timing; it's about the attitude of your heart. It's when your heart is distracted away from God that He becomes grieved, and you may feel as though He is no longer close to you. You can be so preoccupied that you may not notice for days, or even weeks.

Do not miss the point of life! Do not choose the way of the world—an existence built on lists and projects and deadlines. That is the way of works. It only leads to death. Instead, take your life from the wellspring of joy that comes from communing with God. Consider where your life comes from—for wherever you gain your life, it is that thing that will rule it.

There is no real life apart from God—only the illusion of life. Don't be fooled, but be strong in the Lord. It is God's desire to walk with you daily. Focus on Him in the way He focuses on you. It will take time and endurance, but that is the way of genuine life. Hold steadfast, and you will reap an abundance of genuine joy.

DAY 23

To you, O LORD,
I lift up my soul; in you I trust, O my God.
Do not let me be put to shame,
nor let my enemies triumph over me.
No one whose hope is in you
will ever be put to shame.

PSALM 25:1–3

SOME people believe that being unmarried is a shame. For some, to be single is to be less than married. They never really live as long as they are single, because life in their eyes cannot be complete until they marry. Unfortunately, they too often believe that falling in love and getting married will take away their shame. That is a lie. The verse does not say, "No one whose hope is in marriage will ever be put to shame." That is ridiculous. The truth is, no one whose hope is in God will ever be put to shame, whether married or single.

Train your eyes to look straight at God. Do not allow your heart to waver to the right or the left, or else you may lose ground in your faith. Give over to God the longings of your heart. Choose Him as your one true lover, the hope of your life, and let your life be nourished by His embrace. (He always longs to hold you.)

There is no shame in being where you are. In

God's time, He will bring to you gifts that deepen and expand the love in your life. God never wants to keep love from you—God is love. His heart desires that the love in your life be ever-increasing, ever-maturing.

Give Jesus your longings. And let your greatest longing be this: to be found faithful in God's eyes.

DAY 24

But we also rejoice in our sufferings. . . .
ROMANS 5:3

WHEN we follow Jesus, we become like Him— and that is both the prize and the cost of discipleship. For when Jesus walked the earth in the flesh, He lived true to Himself in every way. He loved everyone perfectly. He never lied. He never made an unholy choice. And they killed Him for it. As we follow Jesus, His presence and personality begin to overtake all of our imperfect parts. He takes over our lives, piece by piece; and the more He does, the more we can expect to be pursued by those who want to kill Him.

Are you being persecuted severely? Rejoice! It shows that you have begun to arrive at true Christ-likeness. Are you never persecuted for your faith? Then let this serve as a warning to you. They persecuted Jesus. If they are not persecuting you, as well, then ask yourself: Are you really His servant?

If you will not identify yourself as His property, or swear fealty to His authority and cause, then you have no place wearing His name. But if you do claim His name, then serve Him faithfully, regardless of the cost to you. This will bring you abundant life and abundant suffering. And, contrary to our culture's thought, those two almost always go together.

DAY 25

I came to
you in weakness and fear,
and with much trembling.
My message and my preaching were not
with wise and persuasive words, but
with a demonstration of the Spirit's power.
1 CORINTHIANS 2:3–4

WE will never learn to walk in power until we first learn to walk in weakness. It is not our strength that convinces others to follow Christ. It is God's strength revealed through our weakness that convinces them. Therefore, for God's power to be demonstrated through us, it is necessary that we do not hide our brokenness from others. People in the world hide their weaknesses and always want us to focus on their strengths. But this is upside down and backwards from the way of the Spirit. His strength is perfected through our weakness. So we will not become powerful in God until we learn to boast about our weakness. For it is only when we are weak that we are strong.

You may ask, "But how can I serve the kingdom when I am so weak?" You cannot. But Christ, working through your weakness, can and will, if only you will stop hiding your weaknesses from others. "Christ in you" is the hope of glory—that is, Christ revealed through your unique blend of traits, blemishes, and broken places.

Do not despise your less perfect parts. They are the conduits through which Jesus can be most clearly seen.

DAY 26

Jesus replied,
"If anyone loves me, he will obey my teaching.
My Father will love him, and we will come
to him and make our home with him."
JOHN 14:23

MANY Christians seem to think that the secret to intimacy with God is to constantly seek out emotionally charged encounters with God's presence. They believe that such encounters, if repeated often enough, can draw them into a place of consistent communion with Jesus through the Holy Spirit.

Nothing could be farther from the truth. The manifestation of God's presence is wonderful, and when He reveals His presence to you, do not hesitate to embrace the experience. But He does not reveal Himself for no reason. Do not confuse these experiences with true intimacy. Intimacy with God comes only one way, and that is through obedience.

Do you want to know God as He truly is? Then obey the Word. Obey the Word in the morning when you feel grumpy. Obey the Word at noon when you are hungry, and in the evening when you are tired. Commit yourself to obey Him regardless of how you feel, what you think, or what you want. When you do this, you will discover that you will not have to go searching for God's presence anymore. The Father will seek you out and reveal His love to you. God reveals His presence to anyone He chooses. But He only makes His home with those who obey Him.

*Yet it was the LORD's will to
crush him and cause him to suffer.*
ISAIAH 53:10

DON'T be surprised when the Lord leads you to
a place that crushes you. Do not recoil from God as
though He did something unexpected. Crushing is a
part of redemption, just as death is a part of resurrection. Without death, there is no resurrection. Without
crushing, there is no redemption. It is God's will to
crush you—that is, to crush all the self-life in you.
The crushing is painful, and we never understand its
purpose in the moment. Later we do understand and
realize that the crushing was necessary—but only if
we remain faithful in the process.

God is far more committed to your freedom
than to your comfort. Does it surprise you that He is
willing to allow you to face pain in order to bring you
into freedom? It shouldn't. He was willing to allow
His own Son to die horribly just to give you the
chance to find life. To us, God's love can seem reckless. He is willing to go to great extremes to set us
free—even if those extremes crush us so that He can
remake us in the image of His Son.

When God brings you into crushing circumstances, do not run from His leading. And do not
stop trusting Him. He loves you without question.

He knows precisely how much this is going to hurt. And He also knows His grace is sufficient to the task. Rest in Him unflinchingly. Believe through the pain.

DAY 28

"Woe to him
who quarrels with his Maker,
to him who is but a potsherd
among the potsherds on the ground.
Does the clay say to the potter,
What are you making?
Does your work say, He has no hands?"
ISAIAH 45:9

BE careful complaining to God about your short-comings. For example, someone might say, "Oh, I'm such a disorganized person! Why didn't God give me a more organized brain?" In the world of comparisons, we will always find that we are simply not all that we think we should be. We are too short, too wide, too big, too logical, too emotional, too awkward, too seri-ous, or too flippant. Such comparisons are ridiculous to the angels. From their point of view, we are like a valley of broken potsherds (pottery pieces) all com-plaining because we don't look just like all the other broken potsherds lying around us. We have four sharp edges, but the broken piece next to us has five, so we complain to God. "Why didn't you give me five edges? Don't you love me?" The whole affair is sadly comical, and it totally misses the point besides.

Contrary to the world's opinion of things, our glory as people does not come from being the most talented, the most beautiful, or the most skilled. Instead, our glory comes from being perfected in Christ. Consequently, the more broken we are, the more flaws we possess (whether visible or invisible), the more God's perfecting power can work through us and endow our lives with splendor in Christ. No wonder Paul boasted in his weaknesses. Our flaws are not designed to make us bitter by comparing ourselves to others, but rather to provoke us to look to God. "Those who look to him are radiant" (Psalm 34:5). If you let Him, God will make your flaws beautiful.

DAY 29

"For whoever exalts himself will be humbled, and whoever humbles himself will be exalted."
MATTHEW 23:12

CHRISTIANS often read these words of Jesus and immediately imagine ways God might exalt them externally. Perhaps God will promote them in their workplace like He did Joseph. Perhaps He will call them to some great and noble task for His kingdom, as He did with Moses. But before God exalts us externally, He exalts us internally—that is, He exalts us in the inner life.

To humble yourself before God simply means to look at yourself through God's eyes and agree with His assessment of who you are. When you have truly humbled yourself in this way, life immediately becomes amazingly simple, and every moment is suddenly filled with endless delight. You are a child again. Humility enables you to embrace with joy your absolute dependence on God for everything. This inner transformation always comes before God exalts you externally.

What arena of your life has grown complicated and full of stress? That's the area where hidden pride is lurking somewhere in your soul, urgently demanding that you do all you can to stay in control, achieve success, or protect yourself from harm. Lay down your pride. Humble yourself before God, freely admitting that you are out of control, unable to succeed, and incapable of protecting yourself. Humbling yourself is not a matter of groveling like a worm. God sees you as His beloved child. Agree with Him, and call upon Him to act as your Father.

*Where there is no revelation,
the people cast off restraint.*
PROVERBS 29:18

THINK of an athlete whose coach says to her, "If you work hard enough, you could win the Olympics." That's a wonderful revelation! In response, the athlete places numerous restraints on her life. She cuts out certain frivolous activities (even though she enjoys them). She sets up an aggressive training regimen (even though she doesn't necessarily enjoy it). She stops drinking soft drinks or eating fried foods. Now, soft drinks and fried foods aren't wrong in and of themselves, but the athlete sets them aside on account of the revelation. She wants to be in the Olympics more than she wants her daily serving of fries.

You have received a far greater revelation than any athlete. Jesus lives inside you. And, what's even more amazing, He wants to live through you. But this latter revelation doesn't come to reality automatically. It requires your sanctification.

Sanctification simply means putting restraints on your life for the sake of a greater goal—like forsaking fries to reach the Olympics, only your goal is far bigger. What noble purpose might God use you for? How could He use you to feed the hungry, reach the lost, change the world? How slow we are to choose the higher path, especially when it means we won't be able to satisfy our flesh on a whim anymore. Who knows what noble purposes we miss for the sake of satisfying ourselves?

DAY 31

I have been
crucified with Christ and
I no longer live, but Christ lives in me.
GALATIANS 2:20

THE life of Christ within us was never designed to be flipped on and off like a switch. "Oh, I have to lead this Bible study," you may say, "so I must begin praying for Jesus to speak through me." What about all the other words you have spoken today? Shouldn't Jesus be allowed to speak through you in those circumstances, as well? Of course He should. The entire purpose of this life is to allow the Son of God free reign in our bodies. Once a disciple truly understands this fact, every moment of life becomes extraordinary.

When we understand that the reason for every moment of our existence is to reveal the Son of God, then everyday life becomes a singular adventure. Doing the laundry, paying the bills—all become expressions of worship as we continually strive to let Jesus have His way through us.

No matter what struggle you face—from sickness and persecution to the monotony of doing dishes—victory will come not from mastering the circumstance but from allowing Christ to master you. Whatever your struggle, stop trying to solve the problem so it will go away. Instead, commit yourself to the endeavor of letting Jesus have His way through you in the midst of the struggle. That is the path of the overcomer.

DAY 32

"And do not set your heart on what you will eat or drink; do not worry about it. For the pagan world runs after all such things, and your Father knows that you need them. But seek his kingdom, and these things will be given to you as well."

LUKE 12:29–31

FUNDAMENTALLY, the spirit of poverty stems from a lack of trust in God's love and the consequential preference to trust in money or possessions instead. All in all, it's a rotten way to live—since neither money nor possessions have any real power to protect our hearts from anything, and trusting in them eventually leads people to forsake everything that's truly meaningful in life. Nevertheless, many people, Christians included, trust in money to make them feel safe, or in possessions to give them joy and fulfillment in life. And what do we get for our choice? A life of worry and stress. We never have enough money, so we worry about getting more. And, even if we have millions in the bank, we worry about keeping it safe.

You cannot serve both God and mammon. Period. Either seek God's kingdom for His glory, or seek to build an earthly kingdom for your own glory. But do not deceive yourself by pretending you can seek both.

Of course, I am not saying you can never make money or live in an expensive home. But you should not seek these things. Instead, seek His kingdom. Then, if God wants you to live in a mansion, He will give it to you. But even then, be careful from the start to commit all of your wealth to God. Anything in our lives that is not surrendered to God eventually rises up as an idol to rival His lordship.

*"Do not be afraid, little flock,
for your Father has been pleased
to give you the kingdom."*

LUKE 12:32

THE kingdom of God never comes to us in the way we expect, or in the timing we expect. Some young Christians, however, ask, "What do I have to do to cause God to reveal Himself to me? How can I please Him so that He will bless me?"

Once you ask those questions, you have embarked on a journey of pure frustration. You begin trying things that you hope will please God. You apply "discipline" to spend more time in the Word, serve in the church, or share Christ with your neighbors, all the while hoping that these things will pave the way for God to reveal Himself to you. But those very things actually prevent God from revealing Himself. If He answered you in the way you wanted, you would wrongly believe that you must perform for His approval and His love. He would never allow that. So He waits until you reach exhaustion and shake your fist at heaven—at a God you think has abandoned you despite all your efforts. When you reach that point, only then is God able to begin His work of love in you.

When you come to God, rest assured knowing

that He is delighted beyond your comprehension to reveal Himself to you. We should never spend time in the Word, or share Christ with our neighbors, in order to secure God's blessing. That perspective comes from fear, not faith. Instead, we spend time in the Word and serve others because we believe God's blessing is already secured. "We love because he first loved us" (1 John 4:19).

DAY 34

*"For where your treasure is,
there your heart will be also."*
LUKE 12:34

OFTEN the greatest deceptions in our lives don't come from Satan. They come from our own hearts. We humans are forever full of duplicitous motives. We give money to the poor, convinced that we are acting out of pure compassion, only to boast about our giving in church a few days later. The hypocrite lives in all of us. Recognizing this is the first step toward integrity.

It's important to know your own heart, if for no other reason than the simple fact that God is more concerned about "why" you do a thing than He is about "what" you are doing. It isn't enough (in fact, it's meaningless) to always do the right thing. You must do the right thing with a right motive.

How do you come to know your heart? Begin by discovering what you treasure. What thing in your life could you not survive without? Your money? Your health? Your family? Your reputation? If your treasure rests in your reputation, God will likely bring you into circumstances in which you must choose between your reputation and His will. God wants to bring us all to a place where the only thing we cannot live without is Christ. In everything else, our hearts should say, "That means a great deal to me, but if God should take it away, then so be it. He knows best, and His grace is sufficient."

DAY 35

"Consider how the lilies grow. They do not labor or spin. Yet I tell you, not even Solomon in all his splendor was dressed like one of these."
LUKE 12:27

THE next time you look at the mountains, or the ocean, or the beauty of the land where you live, consider this: You carry a greater measure of God's glory within you than all of these created things combined.

Stop thinking you don't belong or that you don't have what it takes (whatever that means). You have a divine right to be here—you are God's chosen vessel. His Son lives in you. No mountain can make that claim. Just being yourself in Christ is a glorious ministry.

Too often we lose the glory of God in our lives because we try too hard to control the process. Well, we can't. And it's a good thing, too. How terrible it would be if an apple tree had to constantly focus and strain to create apples—it would have little time for anything else.

We are no different. If we had to strain and work in our own strength to reveal God's glory through our lives, we would be constantly exhausted from the effort. Most times, the glory of God is revealed through us when we are totally unaware of it. So the best way to allow God's glory free reign is to develop a heart that is wonderfully unaware of itself, and keenly and consistently aware of God. Focus on Jesus and live with passion. The glory will take care of itself.

For everyone born of God
overcomes the world.
This is the victory that has
overcome the world,
even our faith.

1 JOHN 5:4

FAITH is not just the key to victory. Faith is victory. To believe is to have overcome. Too often Christians say, "I am believing God for a victory" or "I am believing God for a breakthrough," as though faith were like some magic spell that controls the natural world. Certainly, the effect of faith is often the revelation of God's power in the natural world. But the real deliverance of faith doesn't occur in the natural world at all.

When we believe, our faith opens our eyes to see what is truly real—that is, the eternal reality of Christ's lordship over every obstacle we face—and it is through embracing that higher reality that we overcome any hindrance circumstances might place before us.

We live too much in the temporary world. These things are just a shadow, but reality is found in Christ. The life of faith in Jesus is not subject to circumstances—rather, the one who believes is carried above circumstance. So regardless of what is happening in the natural realm, through faith we can rest freely in joy and peace. That is why faith is victory. Faith takes you beyond the reach of temporal circumstances and into the life of Christ, which has already overcome the obstacle you are facing.

The circumstance will change—God will act. But the goal of spiritual growth is to believe in Jesus so completely that when the change does come in the natural world, it is no longer essential to your happiness.

DAY 37

"By standing firm you will gain life."
LUKE 21:19

TRUE faith isn't the capacity to believe that God will work a miracle; it's the tenacity to believe in God's character when He fails to do the miracle you wanted. To stand firm in God means to dig in your heels and cling stubbornly to your confidence in God's character, even when He doesn't meet your obvious need. Others may look at you and say, "Your God has failed you!" But you say with confidence, "My God has not failed me. He has not met the need that I can see, but He cannot be cruel or make mistakes. He must be meeting a greater need I cannot see."

We may come to believe in God because of some

miraculous act He performs. But He never intends for His children to let their faith remain on that immature level. As soon as you begin to grow spiritually, you will find God seeming to step away from your life, or doing some other thing you don't expect. When that test comes, make up your mind to trust in God's character. "I cannot understand what God is doing, but I believe He is a good God, and He loves me. I will trust Him no matter what happens." As soon as you make that conscious choice, your life with Jesus will be lifted to an entirely new level. Through His Spirit, you begin to understand that real life doesn't come through God's actions, but through God Himself. God is looking for people who will believe in Him no matter what. He is testing you to see whether you might be one of them. Are you?

DAY 38

O LORD,
the king rejoices in your strength.
How great is his joy in the victories you give!
PSALM 21:1

IT'S easy to find yourself complaining to God about your weaknesses. But God is not interested in "fixing" you, then sending you on your way; His goal is to complete you. We think we will have joy, if only God would make us strong. But this is not the way of a person who follows after God's heart. "O Lord," David wrote, "the king rejoices in your strength." God is always strong. Pursue intimacy with Him, and you will find you do not care about your weakness anymore. Instead you will find your joy in His unfailing strength.

When God is your strength, you realize that you do not have to be strong anymore. Neither do you have to gain your own victories, but your "joy will be great" in the victories that God gives to you. To be a king (or queen) in God's kingdom, you must understand the paradox that your weaknesses are actually strengths—because your weaknesses are the doorways through which God enters your life. God never establishes intimacy with you on the point of your strength, but on your weakness. It's in the weak places that He completes you with His strength. It's not about being "fixed"; it's about becoming one with Christ.

> *He reached down*
> *from on high and took hold of me;*
> *he drew me out of deep waters.*
> *He rescued me from my powerful enemy,*
> *from my foes, who were too strong for me.*
> *They confronted me in the day of my disaster, but*
> *the LORD was my support. He brought me out into a*
> *spacious place; he rescued me because he delighted in me.*
>
> PSALM 18:16–19

WHEN we are young in our faith, we like to believe we are impervious—that God will never let us face anything that could destroy us. But then reality hits, and we realize that God does not always prevent overpowering enemies from assailing us.

You will never truly perceive God as a great deliverer until these enemies come upon you. But as soon as you abandon denial and see that your enemy is too powerful for you, you cry out to God, just as David did, "Deliver me!" And in that prayer you wrap all of your remaining hope. If God does not answer, if He does not deliver, then you will die.

But your God is determined to set you free and give you victory. He doesn't give victory in the way you might expect or wish, though. Rather than removing you from the pain, He prepares a table before you in the presence of your enemies (Psalm 23:5). He will deliver you, in a way you could never accomplish. Then you will know with confidence that God really loves you, and you will see with your own eyes the irreversible downfall of the enemy who threatened your life.

David never pretended to be stronger than Goliath. But he was willing to confront the giant anyway, because he knew God was with him. In the same way, do not be afraid to confront the giants in your own life. God is with you; He is your great deliverer.

DAY 40

The next day
John was there again with two of his disciples.
When he saw Jesus passing by,
he said, "Look, the Lamb of God!"
When the two disciples heard him say this,
they followed Jesus.
Turning around, Jesus saw them following and asked,
"What do you want?"
They said, "Rabbi. . .where are you staying?"
"Come," he replied, "and you will see."
JOHN 1:35–39

WHEN we first come to Jesus, we often come packed full of questions:

Whom do You want me to marry?

What do You want me to do with my life?

What job should I take?

Where should I live?

But eventually God sifts us down to just one question, the one that really matters, the same one the disciples asked: "Rabbi, where are You staying?"

To grow in Christ means to eventually get to the place where being with Him is all that matters. Jesus is not some two-bit fortune-teller who provides answers on command. He is the answer, and once you learn to abide in Him, all your questions are instantly put to rest.

Examine the questions you ask Jesus, and you will see where you are in your spiritual maturity. Of course God cares about whether you should marry, or whether you should take that particular job offer. But those questions don't even begin to approach the heart of God's will for your life. Ask, "Jesus, where are You staying?" and you will soon find yourself in places you never expected to be, seeing things you never imagined you could see.

What is God's will for your life? Jesus is the Way.

How can you know the right thing to do? Jesus is the Truth.

Where can you find real love and abiding joy? Jesus is the Life.

DAY 41

When they landed,
they saw a fire of burning coals
there with fish on it, and some bread.
Jesus said to them,
"Bring some of the fish you have just caught."
JOHN 21:9–10

ONE of the greatest barriers to stepping out for God is that we insist on waiting around for some great task that's worthy of our calling. But here in these verses the Lord Jesus has been resurrected from the dead, and what does He do? He cooks breakfast for His friends.

Do you believe God has called you to rule nations? Perhaps He has, but you must begin by learning how to rule your own attitude. Have you been called to share Christ in the streets of a foreign country? Then begin by sharing Christ with the child who plays across the street from your front door.

When God plants within your heart a vision for your life, don't assume it's going to come to you prepackaged without any cost or effort on your part. God doesn't plant grand visions within us for our entertainment. He does it to provoke us to grow up. David may have been anointed king when he was still a boy, but he spent many years after that learning how to rule sheep before God would allow him to rule people. Don't despise your small beginnings. What matters is not how grand your vision for the future might be, but how consistent your obedience is in the here and now.

Pay attention to the small things God leads you to do. Sometimes God's love is more powerfully revealed through a hug than through a prophetic word.

DAY 42

*"Greater love has no one than this,
that he lay down his life for his friends.
You are my friends if you do what I command."*
JOHN 15:13–14

ARE you willing to die for Jesus' sake? That is a noble love, but it is not yet the greatest love. The greatest love comes not in dying for Jesus, but in living for Him. Jesus is not saying we should physically die for Him (though He may call some to do that), but rather that we should lay down our lives for Him.

We lay down our lives for Jesus by doing what He commands—but we usually would find it easier to literally die than lay down our control of our lives. To die for a friend is a one-time act of absolute devotion, but to lay down your life for a friend means to die daily, consistently choosing to live every moment for your friend rather than for yourself. By the same token, to live for Jesus is to adopt a life of absolute servitude—a life in which you abdicate all of your rights and live to serve Christ alone. This is why Paul always referred to himself as a "bondslave of Christ"—as a piercing reminder of his choice to love Jesus with the greatest love of all.

Never claim to love God unless you are ready to commit yourself to obedience to Him. "Whoever has my commands and obeys them, he is the one who loves me" (John 14:21). Don't substitute a warm fuzzy feeling for genuine love. There is no way to love God apart from obedience.

DAY 43

*The tongue has
the power of life and death,
and those who love it will eat its fruit.*
PROVERBS 18:21

FEW Christians understand the creative and destructive power of their words. Words have the power to bring life to someone whose heart is dying or dead (including your own heart). And words have the power to kill the life of God within you or someone else.

Don't just avoid gossip; run from it as though running from a plague. For it is a plague and does more damage to the people of God than any other weapon of the enemy. To gossip about others is to curse them. Remember, you will be judged by every careless word you allow to fall out of your mouth (Matthew 12:36–37).

God's Spirit will never lead you to pronounce curses on His children or to sit in the judge's chair. You are called to speak life to people. In every circumstance, strive to let your conversation call forth the life of God in others. Whatever the offense, whatever the justification for anger, make up your mind to speak a blessing, and never, never curse.

I wonder how many Christians have unwittingly destroyed the work of God simply to satisfy their temper.

DAY 44

Do not be
anxious about anything,
but in everything, by prayer and petition,
with thanksgiving, present your requests to God.
And the peace of God, which transcends
all understanding, will guard your hearts
and your minds in Christ Jesus.

PHILIPPIANS 4:6–7

THE peace of God is not just the comfortable recognition of God's presence; it is a powerful defensive weapon. When your heart has no peace, you become an open target for the enemy. That is why, in any spiritual battle, the first thing Satan attacks is your peace. It is your first line of defense. And the loss of peace is always a clear sign that your enemy is at the door.

In these verses Paul is not simply talking about a way to feel okay about life. Instead, he is giving a strategy for warfare:

- Do not accept anxiety. Anxiety is never from God. Examine your life. In what areas are you plagued by anxiety? Those are the avenues through which Satan's attack will come.
- Consciously transfer responsibility for your life to God. This does not mean you should behave irresponsibly. Rather, list the things

that make you feel anxious and purposefully acknowledge God's authority over each thing.

- Develop a thankful heart. Thankfulness inspires our faith and strengthens our capacity to cast our burdens on the Lord.
- Receive God's peace. Notice that it is God's peace you should seek—not your own. Our own peace comes when things around us make sense and go the way we think they should. But God's peace "transcends understanding." That is, His peace isn't based on our circumstance. Enter His peace, and allow it to place a guard over your heart.

DAY 45

The LORD does not look
at the things man looks at.
Man looks at the outward appearance,
but the LORD looks at the heart.

1 SAMUEL 16:7

DON'T make it your ambition to do great things for God; make it your ambition to have a great heart for God—then the "great things" will take care of themselves. You will always have people who try to measure your life by some great act of service or sacrifice. "You are godly if you do this or that." That is pure foolishness—we are not made holy by any "work" we do or don't do. There are multitudes of Christians who do so-called "great deeds" every day, but their hearts are not right. Frankly, God isn't the least bit interested in their great acts of service. Whether you preach to thousands or quietly mop floors means little to Him. What matters to God is the heart.

To grow up in Christ, we must understand that God is far more concerned with our inner lives than He is with our outer lives. That is not to say that you should go off and sin at will. But it does mean you will never grow up as long as you keep putting the cart before the horse. Strive to have a pure, humble, passionate heart for God. Make that your sole ambition. Then you will find yourself doing great things for God without even being conscious of it.

Don't worry about having a great reputation with people. No matter how you live, there will always be some people who accept you, and some who reject you. Instead, continually ask yourself the question that matters: What is my reputation with God?

*Am I now trying to win
the approval of men, or of God?
Or am I trying to please men?
If I were still trying to please men,
I would not be a servant of Christ.*

GALATIANS 1:10

IT is impossible to serve Christ freely and be a "people pleaser" at the same time. Once you have made up your mind to serve Jesus, it won't be long before the Holy Spirit begins to deal with your heart concerning the fear of rejection. Jesus was rejected by the majority of the people He met, and if you follow Him, you can expect the same reaction. " 'No servant is greater than his master' " (John 15:20). If they persecuted Jesus (and they did), then they will persecute you, also. As long as you fear the rejection of others, you will never be able to walk in true freedom in Christ or obey Him with your whole heart.

When we come to God, we all harbor a fear of rejection to one degree or another. When God reveals that fear in you, you must show it no mercy. Never say, "Oh, I worry about offending people. That's just the way I am." No, that's just the way your flesh is. Repent, and obey God in spite of the fear. God does not want you to offend people needlessly, but the very nature of walking in purity with God means that some people around you will be offended.

God is the creator and ruler of the universe. He is the King of kings. He has already proclaimed that you are accepted in Christ. If, then, some people reject you as you strive to follow Him with your whole heart, their issue is not with you but with the King who has accepted you and called you into His service. Defer such people to God and go about your business.

DAY 47

It is for freedom
that Christ has set us free.
Stand firm, then, and do not let yourselves
be burdened again by a yoke of slavery.
GALATIANS 5:1

WE begin to walk with God like children, following His lead in simple faith. But soon other Christians see us walking in a direction that God has never taken them, and they immediately confront us. "You can't do that. God has never led us that way. If you want to please God, you must live like we do."

Beware of those who try to kill the freedom God has given you. Most often, they try to accomplish this by imposing on you their own high-minded religious rules. Such rules are rarely concerned with the obvious "rights and wrongs" of God's Word, but rather focus on all the gray areas in between.

Following Christ is not simply a matter of following rules. (If it were, we would still be under the Law.) Following Christ is a matter of relationship. Where God leads one, He may not lead another. While He restricts one child, He may give another a long leash. That is the glorious freedom of being God's child. We don't have to be clones of one another to be pleasing to God.

Always remember that Jesus set you free for freedom's sake. He delights to see you revel in the glorious freedom He has provided through salvation. So be zealous for your freedom in Christ! Study the Word for yourself and learn to follow the Spirit's direction. Make up your mind to walk in simple and pure devotion to Christ, and beware of anyone who tries to add his or her "rules" to your lifestyle.

DAY 48

You, my brothers, were called to be free.
But do not use your freedom to indulge the sinful nature;
rather, serve one another in love.

GALATIANS 5:13

TRUE freedom is a dangerous thing. One look at Adam and Eve in the Garden can tell us that. God gave them freedom to choose, and the result was the fall of an entire race. Of course, God understood the risk, yet in His sovereignty He decided to give them freedom anyway. Why would God do such a reckless thing? Because He values freedom that much.

Nevertheless, when freedom comes to us in Christ, we must recognize that it doesn't come without danger. God wants you to revel in your freedom, but He never wants for you to flaunt your freedom in a way that undermines love—either love for God or for others.

Perhaps God has given you freedom to do a particular thing, but your brother or sister in Christ is offended when they see you do it. You say, "God has told me it's okay. If they are offended, that's their problem." No, it's your problem, because your attitude is selfish. You are no longer walking in love. Never exalt your freedom above your responsibility to love others.

You were called to be free. So be free. But, more importantly, be loving.

*"If you have raced with men
on foot and they have worn you out,
how can you compete with horses?
If you stumble in safe country,
how will you manage in
the thickets by the Jordan?"*

JEREMIAH 12:5

WE are often surprised when God begins to deliberately subject us to His disciplined training. What surprises us is not that God wants us to be trained, but that the training is so hard. Anyone who follows God for any length of time quickly learns that the Holy Spirit is relentless. He is a master of turning every circumstance, however major or minor, into a training session. Our world becomes God's training gym, and every situation is an opportunity for God to teach us. God's goal is not to wear us out, but to prepare us for the future. At first, the tests God brings may seem difficult, but they are only small tastes of the greater tests you will face in the future.

Never mistake this fact: God's vision for your life is always greater than your own. You may think the tests He brings are extreme, but that is only because your vision for your own life is too small. He wants to make your life extraordinary. Such an extraordinary life requires extraordinary preparation. Ask

God to reveal His "greater vision" for your future, and as soon as He does, you will immediately see that the tests He brings are not extreme at all. If anything, they are gentle compared to the greatness of the vision He holds for your life.

Choose to pursue God's "greater vision" for your life, and do not lose heart in the trials He allows. Remember: The harder the test, the greater the glory.

DAY 50

O LORD, you deceived me,
and I was deceived;
you overpowered me and prevailed.
I am ridiculed all day long; everyone mocks me.
Whenever I speak, I cry out proclaiming violence
and destruction. So the word of the LORD has
brought me insult and reproach all day long.
JEREMIAH 20:7–8

JEREMIAH felt deceived by God, but God never deceived Him. Jeremiah was deceived by his own arrogance. Jeremiah should not have been surprised to find himself in troubling circumstances for God's sake, and neither should we.

We all have our fairy tales about how life with God should be, but all of these fairy tales must die if we are ever to get to know the real Jesus. God is not worried about protecting your fairy tale; He is interested in revealing to you who He really is. Once you begin to pursue the real Jesus, He will immediately begin dismantling your misconceptions about Him. Life in Christ is wonderful—more wonderful than we can imagine—but it is far from what we expect. We will never experience the true wonders of life with Christ unless we first allow Him to crucify our limited vision of who He is.

If you find yourself feeling disillusioned because of where God has taken you (or allowed you to go), then you can be sure that your picture of God is too small. God is graciously guiding you to a place of "more"—more life, more truth, more of Him. When God brings disillusionment to your small picture, don't judge God or accuse Him as Jeremiah did. Instead, willingly lay down your small vision, and ask the Holy Spirit to enlarge your heart so you can discover the grand abundance of life in Christ that you have missed until now.

DAY 51

*The sluggard craves
and gets nothing, but the desires of
the diligent are fully satisfied.*
PROVERBS 13:4

SOME people confuse diligence with workaholism, but the two concepts are nothing alike. Biblical diligence has nothing to do with "making a way for yourself in the world," "pulling yourself up by your own bootstraps," or any form of exertion that encourages you to trust in your natural abilities.

Unlike workaholism, biblical diligence is always closely tied to our faith in God's leadership. We are diligent to do the things that God has told us to do because we trust in His character—and we diligently rely on His grace (that is, His power) to accomplish them. We have no business striving to accomplish tasks that God has never assigned, however noble or advantageous the task may seem to us. Your flesh (or natural abilities) can never lead to a place of success in God's eyes.

When it comes to diligence, it isn't enough to pursue the right things; we must pursue the right things in the right way. When God tells us to do a thing, our first inclination is to snatch the command out of His hand, say thank you, then run off and try to accomplish the task on our own. When we do this, we fail to realize that the process matters far more to God than the end result. Be diligent in the Spirit, applying God's power to accomplish what He has commanded you to do. That alone will lead you to true success.

*What the wicked
dreads will overtake him;
what the righteous desire will be granted.*
PROVERBS 10:24

FEAR is to Satan what faith is to God. Satan always attacks us at the point of our fear. This was true even for Job. "What I feared has come upon me; what I dreaded has happened to me" (Job 3:25). Satan operates in the realm of fear, but God never deals with His children that way. "For God has not given us a spirit of fear" (2 Timothy 1:7 NLT), but "perfect love drives out fear" (1 John 4:18).

Without fear, Satan can gain no foothold. It makes sense, then, to grab hold of every fear in your life and invite God to help you overcome it. How? By asking God for a greater revelation of His love in each area where fear abides. Do you fear rejection or failure or illness or financial ruin? Then ask God to reveal to you His perfect love for you in that area of your life. A sufficient realization of God's love for you will always overcome any fear that plagues your life.

In doing this, of course, I don't mean you should throw out common sense. It is not God's will for you to be afraid of heights, but that doesn't mean you should go leaping off a cliff just to prove your victory. You can have a healthy respect for heights without fearing them. The same principle applies to many things.

But never allow fear to rule your choices in anything you do. Instead, pray for the revelation of God's love, and move forward in faith.

DAY 53

Whoever claims to live in him
must walk as Jesus did.
1 JOHN 2:6

TYPICALLY, we Christians set the bar of our faith far too low. "I know that Jesus did great things and walked in intimate communion with God, but that's because He was the Son of God. You can never expect me to live the way He did." But that is exactly what God expects. "Whoever claims to live in Him must walk as Jesus did."

Well, how did Jesus walk, then? He walked as a man following the leading of God's Spirit—just as we are called to follow the Spirit in Christ. "Your attitude should be the same as that of Christ Jesus: Who, being in very nature God, did not consider equality with God something to be grasped, but made himself nothing, taking the very nature of a servant. . . . He humbled himself and became obedient to death—even death on a cross" (Philippians 2:5–8).

Jesus did nothing in His own strength, but relied on the Spirit's power. Jesus did not follow His own will, but obeyed God's will to the point of death. Jesus did not speak His own words, but spoke only what the Father told Him to speak. All of this is no different from the way we are called to walk with Christ. The only difference is that Jesus walked with God perfectly, something we will never do in this lifetime. But God does not expect you to be perfect; instead He expects you to rely on *His* perfection.

DAY 54

Since, then,
you have been raised with Christ,
set your hearts on things above,
where Christ is seated at the right hand of God.
Set your minds on things above,
not on earthly things. For you died,
and your life is now hidden with Christ in God.
When Christ, who is your life, appears,
then you also will appear with him in glory.
COLOSSIANS 3:1–4

IRONICALLY, it's when we fix our hearts on Jesus—not on ourselves—that we at last come to see our true identity for the first time. The simple reason for this is that our true identity is found in Him—and nowhere else. Outside of Christ, it is impossible for us to truly know ourselves.

As you fix your heart on Jesus, the first thing He will begin to do is expose in you all of the false ways you try to establish your identity. Perhaps you define yourself by your success in business, by the money you make, or by the people you date. Or perhaps you define yourself in subtler ways—for example, by finding ways to be needed, or making sure you're the "funny one" in your circle of friends. However you try to define yourself outside of Christ, God will root out your method and expose it plainly. He will demand that you "die" to every false identity you have—so that your true identity in Christ can begin to be revealed.

Do not be fooled into thinking this process is easy, for it is anything but. The dying can be endured as long as we keep in mind what God is accomplishing for us—the revelation of who we are meant to be in Christ. "Let us fix our eyes on Jesus, the author and perfecter of our faith, who for the joy set before him endured the cross" (Hebrews 12:2).

DAY 55

Now the Lord is the Spirit,
and where the Spirit of
the Lord is, there is freedom.
2 CORINTHIANS 3:17

FREEDOM is one of the great ways to identify God's Spirit at work in a person or a church. Whenever you encounter people who are walking in the fullness of God's Spirit, one of the first things you notice about them is that they are free, and that their freedom seems to be neither defined nor controlled by their circumstances. That's because their freedom is supernatural—delivering them from a life of law to one of grace. "Because through Christ Jesus the law of the Spirit of life set me free from the law of sin and death" (Romans 8:2). This freedom is only experienced by those who are willing to let go of their own control and continually submit themselves to the day-to-day work of God's Spirit within them.

Of course, the lack of freedom in a person or a church is also a clear signal that God's Spirit is conspicuously absent. I do not mean to suggest that God's Spirit is not omnipresent—only that the work of His Spirit is often hindered in people or in places where you'd think it would be the most free—namely, in Christians and their churches.

Wherever God's Spirit is manifested, there is freedom. Does your life lack that supernatural sense of freedom? Is there some area of your life that is still tied up in oppression? What about your local assembly—does it shine as a beacon of freedom? Identify the areas that are not free and ask God to shine the light of His Spirit on them.

DAY 56

"I am the way."
JOHN 14:6

THERE once was a missionary who lost his way while trying to reach a village in the jungles of

Africa. After wandering for some time, he came upon a small hut with a family inside resting in the midday heat. Cautiously, he approached to ask whether any of them could help him find his destination. The father, who was familiar with the area, offered to lead him to the village he sought.

For more than an hour, the missionary followed the man, hacking their way through the jungle's thick growth. Eventually, the missionary began to wonder whether the man really knew where he was going.

"Are you sure this is the way?" the missionary asked.

"Yes," said the native.

"But where is the path?" the missionary asked.

The native stopped and said, "In this place, there is no path. I am the path."

What the native said to the missionary is the same thing Jesus says to us every day: "In this world, there is no path. I am the path." But, like the missionary, we prefer to travel on paths that we can easily see and follow unaided. That way, we have little need for faith, and absolutely no need for a guide. But you are called to "walk by faith, not by sight."

DAY 57

"I am. . .the truth."
JOHN 14:6

YOU cannot confront Christ without also confronting the truth, because Jesus is the truth. And sooner or later Christ the Truth points His gaze directly at you—your heart, your motives, your secret ambitions—and He reveals some dark truth about your fallen heart. Such revelations are hard to take. When Jesus begins to deal in this way, many Christians push Him away to a "safer" distance, where they can still pretend to serve Christ while continuing to ignore the darkness in their own souls. Those who do this fail to realize that the very truth they run from is the truth that will set them free.

When Jesus shines the light of truth on some black part of your soul, do not dispute the revelation. Do not run from it. Do not ignore it. Do not say, "Well, that's just the way I am, and there's nothing to be done." There is something to be done: You must embrace the truth about yourself. You must accept the truth about yourself. But, even more, you must believe the truth of Christ in you.

Jesus never reveals truth for no reason. His purpose is to provoke a transformation within us—a transformation that changes us into the image of Christ. No matter what dark problem Christ reveals within you, you can rest in the fact that God can take whatever darkness you have and transform it to reflect His image. That is the truth that sets you free.

THERE is no life outside of Christ. This truth is simple enough to understand cognitively, but it can take entire lifetimes for the understanding to reach our hearts. All that is life—all that is truly meaningful, all that is truly alive, all that is truly fulfilling, all that is truly rich and full of joy—is contained in Christ.

There are many things in this world that pretend to be life. People take drugs because they make them feel "alive." People dive off cliffs, or ski down mountains, because the adrenaline rush makes them feel "alive." People pursue careers, compete as athletes, play the stocks, and build families, all because they believe such things can give them the good "life." But none of these things in and of themselves truly brings life. Apart from Christ, all such pursuits are meaningless.

The Word is clear—real life is found in Christ and nowhere else. This is wonderful news for the single person who is desperate to get married, the person who thinks that marriage and family are what give life meaning. You do not need to pine after marriage as though it were the only thing that could bring meaning to your life. If you continue on that road, you will be deeply disappointed whether you eventually get married or not. Jesus is accessible now—and He is eager to show you what real life is all about.

DAY 59

He who guards
his mouth and his tongue
keeps himself from calamity.
PROVERBS 21:23

GOD'S power is contained in His words. Genesis tells us that "God spoke. . .and it was so"— and we are created in God's image. It follows, then, that our "spiritual power" is also contained in our words. (The Scripture strongly supports this fact. Take a look at James 3:3–8; Proverbs 10:11; 13:3; and 18:7, to name a few.)

When we line up our words to agree with God's Word, we will experience a continual flow of God's power. When our words don't line up with God's truth—well, there's power in that, too, but it's a negative power rather than a positive one. "The tongue also is a fire, a world of evil among the parts of the body. It corrupts the whole person, sets the whole course of his life on fire, and is itself set on fire by hell" (James 3:6).

Words hold power, and you reap the fruit of your words as surely as you reap the fruit of your physical labor. With our words we bless God, but then we turn around and curse what God loves. We may curse ourselves: "Oh, I'm just a failure at everything I try. I'll never amount to anything." Or we may curse others through gossip or private judgments: "That guy is a selfish jerk. He doesn't care about anything or anyone but himself."

Examine your speech. What are you blessing these days? And what are you cursing? Watch your words carefully. They have real power for good or evil.

DAY 60

*He makes me
lie down in green pastures,
he leads me beside quiet waters.*
PSALM 23:2

THE "green pastures" and "quiet waters" David speaks of here have nothing to do with circumstances.

David was writing about an internal reality. Though he walked through the valley of the shadow of death, he feared nothing. He was not living under the reign of circumstance.

Are you thirsting for "quiet waters" in your own life? Then do not waste time looking for a change in circumstance. A new job won't do it. A vacation won't do it. A new relationship won't do it. All of these are just Band-Aids that temporarily cover the wound.

The only lasting "green pastures" and "quiet waters" are found in the heart, gifts of the Holy Spirit. Nothing in circumstance can create them, nor maintain them. Such unshakeable peace springs only from your union with Christ. And, once you submit to Jesus as your shepherd, He will always lead you to peaceful places where your soul can rest undisturbed continually. Continually.

Regardless of what happens around you, your good shepherd wants you to remain beside the quiet waters of His presence. God wants you to be free from concern, unshakeable, fearless, and always at ease. Such an extraordinary condition does not come from peaceful circumstances; it comes from drawing your reality from a wholly different source. Let the peace of Christ rule in your heart, and your circumstances will cease to be an issue.

*May God himself,
the God of peace,
sanctify you through and through.
May your whole spirit, soul and body be kept
blameless at the coming of our Lord Jesus Christ.
The one who calls you is faithful and he will do it.*
1 THESSALONIANS 5:23–24

TO be sanctified means to be set apart for a special purpose or a special person. A bride is to remain sanctified (set apart) for her husband. On the day he comes to marry her, she prepares herself in joy. She adorns herself with splendor. She is radiant and radiates the delight of her love. She has paid a price for this union. She has remained "set apart" for the sake of her beloved—so that they can be together with nothing to hinder their intimacy.

In a similar way, Jesus wants us to be set apart for Him. The process of sanctification will gradually heighten your sensitivity to impurity. If you are constantly covered in mud, then slapping another wad of dirt on your face can seem trivial. But once God begins to clean you off, then that same wad of dirt stands out like a nasty stain, and spoils your whole appearance.

Don't be surprised when God begins to ask you to stop doing something you've been doing freely for years. He may have allowed it until now, but if you are to be fully sanctified for Him, then that thing (however trivial it may seem to your mind) must go. Don't resist God's sanctifying work in your life, but understand that God is preparing you for an intimate union with Himself. Never make the foolish mistake of choosing a selfish vice over intimacy with God.

DAY 62

Rather, clothe yourselves
with the Lord Jesus Christ,
and do not think about how to gratify
the desires of the sinful nature.
ROMANS 13:14

RELATIVELY minor things can divert you from your true course—even some things that once seemed ordinary and mundane. For example, not getting to bed on time, watching television when there are more productive things to be done, or saying something negative about a friend (even if you say it under your breath where no one but you and God can hear)—all of these simple things can become ways we might put off Christ in order to "gratify the desires of the sinful nature." You can be denied the true fullness of walking with Christ by something as common as procrastination.

Romans 13:14 provides a specific strategy for staying on the true path of discipleship:

1. Clothing yourself in Christ is the only goal with which you ever need to be concerned. To wear Jesus as a garment means to put on His character and take on His mission. It means to cover your identity with Christ, to wrap your soul with His Spirit, to saturate your life with Him in such a way that whoever looks at you will mistake you for Jesus. To overcome the flesh, this must be your primary focus in life.

2. Once your focus is firmly set, you can overcome the sinful nature simply by ignoring it and making no provision for its desires. In this way, you will essentially starve it into submission.

DAY 63

"My people have committed two sins:
They have forsaken me, the spring of living water,
and have dug their own cisterns,
broken cisterns that cannot hold water."
JEREMIAH 2:13

OUR God is the "spring of living water." But coming to Him will do you no good unless you come as a child—joyfully acknowledging your utter dependence on God for everything, and implicitly trusting Him to provide for you in every circumstance. Coming to God in this way is not easy be-cause the sinful nature within us rejects the very notion of childlike faith. To the reasoning flesh, such faith appears ludicrous. So, instead of coming to drink from the fountain of living water, our sinful nature would always prefer to grab a shovel and work to exhaustion digging wells of its own design—wells that always, inevitably, dry up.

Are you spiritually weak? Does your heart feel dull and thirsty? Perhaps you are exhausted from digging dry wells of your own. Where do you go to give your soul a drink? That is, to whom or what do you turn when you feel empty, directionless, or out of control? If your answer is "Jesus," that's well and good. But if your answer is something other than Jesus, then you are in for a frustrating time. For no matter where you run, or to whom you turn, you will never find true living water anywhere outside of Christ. Only He can truly satisfy.

Then Peter came to Jesus and asked,
"Lord, how many times shall
I forgive my brother when he sins against me?
Up to seven times?" Jesus answered,
"I tell you, not seven times, but seventy-seven times."

MATTHEW 18:21–22

YOU can be certain of this one thing: If you commit your heart to follow Christ, He will eventually test your resolve to walk in His steps—that is, to walk in forgiveness. Perhaps the test will come when someone commits an unspeakable sin against you, one that drives a spear deep into your heart and drives you to scream at heaven, "This is too much!" But, more likely, the test will come to you as it did to Peter—through a brother or sister who habitually sins against you in smaller ways. "How many times do I have to forgive this person before it's too much? I want to forgive, but I won't let myself become a doormat for someone to walk all over." This was Peter's cry, as well—how much forgiveness is enough? Surely there is a limit.

Jesus' response tells us there should be no limit to forgiveness. It's terrifying to think we have to extend forgiveness repeatedly and without limit toward those who habitually injure us. After all, isn't that being "co-dependent"? But God is not codependent, nor is He self-abusive, allowing us to "walk all over Him." The very notion is ridiculous. And yet His mercy is never ending. God forgives us because He is gracious, and He loves us. He forgives us not because He is weak, but because He is strong. To follow Him means that we, too, must be filled with His strength and grace— and that we, too, must forgive freely, even (and especially) when it really hurts us to do so.

DAY 65

Therefore, as God's chosen people, holy and dearly loved, clothe yourselves with compassion, kindness, humility, gentleness and patience. Bear with each other and forgive whatever grievances you may have against one another. Forgive as the Lord forgave you.
COLOSSIANS 3:12–13

YOUR identity in Christ supercedes your identity as a man or a woman. "There is neither. . .male nor female, for you are all one in Christ Jesus" (Galatians 3:28). I am not saying that no differences exist between men and women. Of course they do, and those differences should be honored. But gender-based divisiveness should have no place in the body of Christ. In Christ, we are one, and we are called to walk in unity. Issues such as gender, race, nationality, and social status must never be used to define our value in the church.

For this reason, it is a sin for you to pass a judgment on a man simply because he is a man. If a man is a member of God's household, the fact that he is a man is secondary—and in no way makes him less capable of understanding the mysteries of intimacy with Christ and His body.

In the same way, it is sin for you to pass judgment on a woman simply because she is a woman. She is a child of God, just like you. The fact that she is a woman will be irrelevant in eternity.

Make it your ambition to bless one another in all things, whether "Jew or Greek, slave or free, male or female, for you are all one in Christ." Let your behavior be shaped, not by the expectations placed on your gender, but rather by the Word of God.

DAY 66

Do not be misled:
"Bad company corrupts good character."
1 CORINTHIANS 15:33

YOU are commanded to love everyone, but you are not commanded to be friends with everyone. It is foolish to believe that, as a Christian, you must befriend everyone who comes across your path. The Bible does not teach such nonsense.

The crux of the issue is this: Bad company corrupts good character. If you set your standards for friendship low, before long you will allow "bad company" to traffic in the inner circle of your life. They will gain access to your heart, and they will wear down your spirit. They will not understand what they see; they will judge you in ridiculous ways; and they will tempt you to think like they think, and to see the world through their own selfish lenses.

Do not think that remaining in friendships like that somehow honors God. On the contrary, God's Word speaks thus: "Above all else, guard your heart, for it is the wellspring of life" (Proverbs 4:23). Love freely, give freely, forgive freely. But be cautious in friendship. Friends have access to your heart. Be sure the friends you choose will guard your heart as faithfully as they guard their own.

*If you, O LORD, kept a record of sins,
O LORD, who could stand?*

PSALM 130:3

MERCY begets mercy. If we truly understood God's mercy, we would never snap at others when they cut in front of us in traffic, nor accuse our co-workers of wrong motives behind their backs, nor get angry with a roommate who never cleans up the kitchen. When we see how much mercy we receive from our holy God, then it suddenly becomes easy to extend mercy to others.

Every silent judgment you make against your brother or sister, every selfish motive that guides your choices, every careless word that comes out of your mouth—all of these rise like a stench in God's nostrils. I say this not to discourage you, but to encourage you to consider the greatness of God's mercy. You will never be perfect before God outside of Christ. But in Christ, God's mercy is always perfect toward you.

So when you feel compelled to curse the fellow who took your parking space, bring this fact to your mind: You have no room to judge. If it weren't for God's mercy pouring all over you right now, you would be in bad shape. If God is willing to extend mercy to you, shouldn't you, then, be willing to pass His mercy on to others when they offend you?

DAY 68

Therefore, brothers, since
we have confidence to enter the Most Holy Place
by the blood of Jesus, by a new and living way
opened for us through the curtain, that is, his body,
and since we have a great priest over the house
of God, let us draw near to God with a sincere heart
in full assurance of faith, having our hearts
sprinkled to cleanse us from a guilty conscience
and having our bodies washed with pure water.
Let us hold unswervingly to the hope we profess,
for he who promised is faithful.
HEBREWS 10:19–23

IN the beginning of our spiritual lives, we do not yet trust in God's character fully. We secretly wonder whether He will come through for us, whether He really loves us, even whether He knows who we are in the great mass of humanity. But we eventually come to see that God is good, that He is loving, that He does know us intimately, and that He is fully capable of delivering His people out of any and every bondage. But we also come to see something else about God—something far more awesome. He is holy. Above all else, He is holy.

In the moment we see His holiness (or even a glimpse of it) for the first time, we instantly understand the huge contradiction inherent in God's love toward us. For this great One who loves us should, in all reasonable logic, be our executioner. We are murderers of God's Son. We are selfish, foolish, unholy, fallen, rebellious beings. And this awesome, white-hot holy God, in whose presence we should be instantly destroyed, has instead chosen to wrap His holiness in human flesh to build a bridge between us. "Our God is a consuming fire," but, through Christ's blood, we have each become a singular, miraculous burning bush. The fire that should consume us, does not. Instead, we are bearers of His glory.

It takes great courage and faith for us to come boldly to God, when you understand this profound reality—that He is fire, and you are wood.

DAY 69

*So I sent
messengers to them with this reply:
"I am carrying on a great project and cannot
go down. Why should the work stop while
I leave it and go down to you?"*
NEHEMIAH 6:3

WHETHER you are aware of it or not, God has called you to a great work. For Nehemiah, that work was to rebuild the walls of Jerusalem. For you and me, it is something far less tangible to human eyes. The great work we are all called to is to develop a "great heart" for God. This is the greatest work for every Christian. Nothing is more important. That's right—nothing matters more to God than the condition of your heart before Him.

Now I will tell you a secret. Many Christians spend the best years of their lives striving to "do great things for God." But despite their great efforts, they end up missing God entirely in the process. They do not understand that God's point in sending Christ was not so that we could do great things for Him, but so that we could know Him. God is all about relationship—that is His passion. And it should be our passion as well.

So, as you seek the Lord in your life, remember this secret: Do not worry yourself with striving to "do great things for God." Instead, always make it your ambition to have a great heart for God. If you do this, you'll find that the "great works" will take care of themselves.

So I sent
messengers to them with this reply:
"I am carrying on a great project and cannot
go down. Why should the work stop while
I leave it and go down to you?"
NEHEMIAH 6:3

NEHEMIAH'S response reflects the attitude we should all have concerning the things that God has laid on our hearts to do. If your heart is dedicated to God (as we discussed yesterday), is God calling you now to a specific great project? Is it to spend some extended time with Him? To do some act of service for your neighbors or your coworkers? To visit those in prison or the sick? Whatever God is asking of you, you must make that thing a nonnegotiable in your life.

What Nehemiah says here is worth committing to memory—and then using it anytime someone tries to distract you from the thing God is calling you to do. We so easily sacrifice what is best for what is good. For instance, it's good to spend time with friends, and there is a time and place for it. But when God calls you away to spend time with Him, you must heed His call at the expense of all other options.

Remember, God is a God of simplicity. Choose the thing He has put before you, and let nothing distract you from that singular purpose. Stay simple. Your friends may not understand you. Your family may even call you selfish for saying no to their desires. But stay true to the great thing God has called you to pursue. In time, the fruit of your life will show that you made the right choice. For wisdom is proved right by her deeds (Matthew 11:19).

DAY 71

Meanwhile, the people in Judah said,
"The strength of the laborers is giving out,
and there is so much rubble
that we cannot rebuild the wall."
NEHEMIAH 4:10

IN some ways, your life is a lot like Jerusalem when the walls fell. Rebuilding may seem like a hopeless and overwhelming task. So take a look at what Nehemiah did, and consider how you can follow his example of extraordinary faith.

- Place a guard over the broken places in your life (Nehemiah 4:13). Do whatever it takes to protect your wounded areas from further attack. Give yourself the gift of a "safe space."
- Place the responsibility for your deliverance in God's hands (Nehemiah 4:14). God never

asks you to deliver yourself, that's His arena of expertise. All He asks is that you relinquish control and place your hope and trust in Him.

- Begin the work (Nehemiah 4:15). What you could never do in your own strength, God is able to do through you, in His strength. It is this cooperation between your obedience and God's power that forms the foundation of true communion with the Holy Spirit. It is "Christ in you" that is "the hope of glory." God may use your hands to pick up the fallen stones, but it will be His strength and wisdom that rebuild the wall.

DAY 72

*"Sanctify them by the truth;
your word is truth."*
JOHN 17:17

YOU can't always trust your experience to know what is true about a person or circumstance. A child's experience of a father's abuse may teach her that all men are untrustworthy. But that is not the truth. A man's experience of a friend's betrayal may teach him that being vulnerable with others is a weakness. But that is not true, either. You cannot construct your view of the world on the basis of your experience. If you do, you will find yourself deceived by your own experience.

By the same token, you can't always trust your sincerity to protect you from being deceived. It is good to develop a passion for the things you believe, but your deep conviction does not guarantee that they are right. The Puritans were a God-fearing people, but their sincerity did not keep them from the horror of the witch-hunts that killed dozens of innocent people. Your passionate conviction does not make you right.

That is not to say you should never listen to the lessons of experience, or to the voice of your own conscience. That would be silly. Rather, be sure you continually test your experiences, your passions, and your convictions against the authority of God's Word. His Word will lead you to the truth—and nothing else.

DAY 73

But you have come. . .to Jesus the mediator of a new covenant.
HEBREWS 12:22, 24

HOW strange that we who profess to love Jesus are so hesitant to meet with Him openly and honestly.

But, then again, perhaps it's not as strange as we might imagine. Most of us rarely meet honestly even with ourselves, much less God. We typically don't take time to look deeply into our hearts because there are ugly things there we wish to avoid.

Perhaps you are lonely and longing for a husband or a wife. But you shove your loneliness deep into the dark recesses of your heart until it becomes a distant dull ache in the back of your mind that has no name. Or perhaps you are able to shove it so deep that you don't even think about it at all. Do we avoid meeting with Jesus "heart to heart" because we don't want Him to see the things we're hiding—or because we don't want to see them ourselves?

I suspect that most often it is the latter. Jesus loves us, even with our ugliness and sin. He is always ready to forgive and extend His healing love to our hearts—but we are not so quick to love ourselves.

Unfortunately, many Christians would rather survive than truly live, because to live we must come to Jesus and lay everything bare before Him. And, for some of us, the cost of that act is higher than we are willing to pay.

What about you? Do you dare to unpack your heart before Him?

DAY 74

Do not merely listen to the word,
and so deceive yourselves.
Do what it says.
JAMES 1:22

MANY Christians deceive themselves into thinking the Word of God is something less than what it is. They treat God's Word as though it were merely a great book of stories, or a book of sage advice, or a book of history.

Of course, the Bible is all of these things. But it is also something much more. It is God's instruction book for how we should live. If we look at God's Word in that light, it becomes a very dangerous book indeed. To obey God's Word is to turn the world around us upside down.

"Love your enemies, do good to those who hate you" (Luke 6:27).

"Forgive as the Lord forgave you" (Colossians 3:13).

"Give to everyone who asks you, and if anyone takes what belongs to you, do not demand it back" (Luke 6:30).

"But when you give a banquet, invite the poor, the crippled, the lame, the blind" (Luke 14:13).

"Do not be overcome by evil, but overcome evil with good" (Romans 12:21).

They are such nice-sounding words, until we realize that God meant for us to obey them. And so we say, "Oh, that's not practical! Jesus must be exaggerating to make a point." Beware of your own intellectual defenses. It's not in the knowing of God's Word, but in the doing of it, that makes a Christian real. Anything less and you are deceiving yourself.

DAY 75

To the pure, all things are pure,
but to those who are corrupted and do not believe,
nothing is pure. In fact, both their
minds and consciences are corrupted.

TITUS 1:15

DO you want to know how to gauge the purity of your heart? Then look at how quick you are to accuse others of unhealthy motives. Someone arrives late to pick you up for an outing, and you suspect she is taking you for granted. Another fails to call you after telling you he would, and you suspect he doesn't care about you as much as he says he does. One person seems hesitant to be open with you, and you suspect she is a snob. Another shares more than you want, and you suspect he is needy.

The pure heart is not burdened with such foolish

speculations. "To the pure, all things are pure." That is not to say that those with pure hearts are naïve—only that they are naturally prone to believe the best about others long before they suspect the worst.

"No," you say, "I'm not being suspicious! I'm using discernment." Perhaps. But before presuming to discern the hearts of others, have you taken the time to discern the condition of your own heart? Is your discernment motivated by a pure love for others? Does your discernment release you to see the good in your friends? Is your sole passion to see your brothers and sisters reach their potential in Christ? Don't make the mistake of disguising a suspicious spirit under the label of "spiritual discernment." Without a pure heart, your discernment cannot be trusted.

DAY 76

We continually remember
before our God and Father your work produced
by faith, your labor prompted by love, and your
endurance inspired by hope in our Lord Jesus Christ.
1 Thessalonians 1:3

YOU will never experience the fullness of life in Christ without first embracing the principle of endurance. Endurance is the simple, profound commitment to pursue and obey Christ's commands whatever the cost, whatever may come. No excuses, no compromise. Endurance takes you to the land of "no matter what." No matter what, I will serve Him. No matter what, I will trust Him. No matter what, I will follow Christ alone.

When we first make the commitment to endure "at any cost," our minds are often filled with images of harsh persecution, rejection from friends or family, or some other extreme hardship. We imagine ourselves as daring champions of Christ's cause, willing to lay down our lives in noble gestures of devotion. But the real test of endurance doesn't come through grand gestures but rather through quiet, consistent commitment.

The great battles of the spiritual life are not fought on the mountaintops of spiritual revelation, but in the lowlands of monotony. The real victory of life in Christ comes when we are willing to obey even when no one is looking and obedience seems pointless. It's one thing to boldly proclaim your willingness to die for Christ, but it's quite another to faithfully seek Him as you do the laundry, pay your bills, mop your floor, or buy your groceries. Commit yourself to that kind of endurance, and you will find Jesus revealing Himself to you in extraordinary ways, even in the most common of circumstances.

DAY 77

*"But blessed is the man who
trusts in the LORD, whose confidence is in him.
He will be like a tree planted by the
water that sends out its roots by the stream.
It does not fear when heat comes;
its leaves are always green.
It has no worries in a year of drought
and never fails to bear fruit."*
JEREMIAH 17:7–8

GOD never promises that you will not have to endure seasons of drought. On the contrary, He assures us such droughts will come. Droughts of loneliness or discouragement. Droughts of disappointment or failure. Droughts of disillusionment or rejection. All these will happen to you somewhere along the path you walk, and some of these droughts may last quite long.

That being said, the greatest danger for our hearts in desert times is not the desert itself but what the desert tempts us to think about God. Make this fact sure in your heart: You are not in the desert because God is evil, or because He doesn't care. In fact, the opposite is true. In the spiritual walk, the desert is the place where we can truly fall in love with Christ. He has removed all distractions, including those that originally made you think you loved Him.

The veil is torn away. Now it's just your naked self, alone with God. Will you choose to love Him now, when He comes to you with no gift to offer except Himself?

The deepest communion with God is always founded in the midst of life's droughts. It is a shame so many people miss their grand love affairs with God because they can't stop complaining long enough about the dryness to notice He is there with them in the desert.

DAY 78

Even my close friend, whom I trusted,
he who shared my bread,
has lifted up his heel against me.
PSALM 41:9

AT some point in the course of your relationships, someone you love will betray you. Few things will cut more deeply or reveal more about your character. For when we have shared secrets with someone, we have the power to deeply injure that person in return. We have eaten together; we have told stories. And when someone like that turns his or her back on us, we have the power to strike deeply; we can hurt as we have been hurt. We can get even.

The great challenge is in choosing not to—and, instead, allowing forgiveness to rule your attitude. "Bless those who persecute you. . . . Bless, and curse not." Let love prevail. The only antidote for the bitterness of betrayal is compassion. So you must make a painful and difficult choice. If you are to bless the person who has betrayed you, you must choose to work toward understanding your betrayer. . .until compassion flows from your heart toward that person.

It is only in loving your betrayer's heart that you will free yourself from bitterness.

DAY 79

But thanks be to God,
who always leads us in triumphal procession
in Christ and through us spreads everywhere
the fragrance of the knowledge of him.
2 CORINTHIANS 2:14

CHRISTIANS often use this verse to shore up their confidence in a God that will eventually lead them to triumph over a particular struggle they face. But that isn't what the verse says at all. God is not promising to make us triumphant over our problems or our foes. He is promising that He will always triumph over us!

The image Paul paints in this passage is that of a Roman emperor leading a procession of captured slaves through the streets of the capital city. God is the emperor. We are, and always will be, His captured slaves. Be thankful! He may well lead you to victory over the obstacles you face. But first He must accomplish His absolute victory over you.

God will never give you your own personal victory over anything. Instead, He gives you His victory. After the dark night of battle against your enemy, God will make sure that you are the only one left standing. But when the battle ends, it will not be the scent of your own sweat and blood that lingers in the air. It will be the Lord's sweet fragrance. The battle has been His all along. He may have fought it through you, but the victory still belongs to Him.

Against every enemy you face, God will fight through you. But never let that fool you into thinking that you are the one fighting.

DAY 80

"Therefore come out
from them and be separate, says the Lord.
Touch no unclean thing, and I will receive you."
"I will be a Father to you,
and you will be my sons and daughters,
says the Lord Almighty."
Since we have these promises, dear friends,
let us purify ourselves from everything
that contaminates body and spirit,
perfecting holiness out of reverence for God.
2 CORINTHIANS 6:17–7:1

THE kingdom of God resides wherever His rule and reign are manifested. For His kingdom to reside in your life, then, you must establish a space around your heart where His authority reigns supreme. You need to create a circle around yourself that is yours and God's alone—a space that filters out the cluttered noise of common life and the droning chatter of everyday concerns. Once established, this "sphere of life" will allow you the freedom to move easily through the world with others, without fear of choking on worldly concerns or buckling under the stress of worldly judgments hurled against you.

Within that holy, sacred atmosphere, you are not known as a professional or a parent or a leader of anyone. In that space (where what is most true reigns), you are just the Father's child. Wherever the kingdom of God is manifested, these revelations quickly become the most obvious facts in the world.

Keep yourself encompassed by the life that comes from Christ—fiercely guarding the "space" around your heart where He alone reigns free. Then your life will be true in every way. No matter what happens outside the sphere, you will not be shaken.

Wherever you go, consciously carry the kingdom of God with you. This does not mean you will escape from the world. Instead, you will be able to live in the world while not becoming a part of it.

DAY 81

"For whoever wants to save his life will lose it, but whoever loses his life for me will find it."
MATTHEW 16:25

THE paradox of losing your life to find it might best be understood this way: Imagine a raging river full of white-water swirls and smooth, dark boulders that cause the current to twist and churn. Now imagine yourself taking a running leap into the center of the current, plunging yourself into the torrent of rushing waters, and experiencing, as a result, an absolute loss of control. In the beginning, that is how it feels to lose your life in

Christ. It's a sort of "baptism unto death," if you can picture it that way. But that is just the beginning.

Once caught in the flow, once the shock of the water enveloping you with such force begins to subside, you soon stop your struggle against the current and, quite suddenly, you find that you are more alive than you have ever been. It is a wild, even reckless, life, but the river flows with a purpose you can only faintly imagine, toward a goal that you cannot see. In joy, you give yourself to the river and, at last, you rest. . .allowing this power so much greater than yourself to take over the details of your existence. And in that rest—that Sabbath rest—you find yourself at peace, sustained and moved by the river to which you have given yourself, fully and without compromise.

The only way to true freedom and self-discovery is through absolute surrender and abandonment to the river that is God. This is the paradox that leads to life.

DAY 82

For the mind set on the flesh is death,
but the mind set on the Spirit is life and peace.
ROMANS 8:6, NAS

TO the mind set on the Spirit, even the most mundane tasks of everyday life take on a holy aspect. Of course, this sounds ridiculous to our natural reasoning. "How can paying the bills or cutting the vegetables for dinner be seen as a 'holy' act? Surely there are some things in life that are spiritually neutral—neither holy nor evil."

Sadly this sort of reasoning bars many Christians from experiencing a deeper walk with God. The real truth of the matter can be seen this way: When you enter a dark room, all the objects in it are cloaked in darkness. The desk, the chair, the bed—they are all dark and indistinct. But when you flip the switch, the room is flooded with light. Darkness flees, as it must (since darkness, by definition, is simply the absence of light). But that doesn't mean that objects that were shrouded in darkness also flee. The desk, the chair, and the bed are all still there, just as they were. It's only that the darkness that covered them is now gone. Now they are shrouded in light. They are crisp and clear, reflecting the luminous energy that shines upon them.

So it is with the mundane aspects of daily life. When we invite our holy God to saturate our lives with His presence, then His light shines on everything we do—sanctifying even the most monotonous tasks we all must perform in order to survive. The laundry will always be with us, but doing the laundry can become a holy act by the simple act of inviting God to do it with us.

DAY 83

"I know your deeds,
that you are neither cold nor hot.
I wish you were either one or the other!
So, because you are lukewarm—neither hot
nor cold—I am about to spit you out of my mouth."
REVELATION 3:15–16

MANY Christians who say they love Jesus do so only from a distance. They are loathe to get too close to Him, lest they be confronted with the depth of their own self-centeredness or find themselves unwittingly identified with Christ as a radical, a militant, or insane—all labels that Christ bore (and continues to bear wherever He shows up).

You can always tell these "fringe" Christians by the simple fact that they are almost indistinguishable from the world around them. They are nondescript and blurry people. . .claiming to possess a supernatural life in Christ, but ultimately living just like everyone else.

These nondescript Christians have built their lives on a secret lie. I say it is "secret" because they would never admit that they believe such a lie—not even to themselves. The lie says this: "When it comes to following Jesus, the prize is not worth the cost." Despite the lie's utter silliness, many, many people believe it and give it power. And, as a result, their lives are powerless.

Let me assure you of this one truth: In your walk with Christ, the prize always, always outweighs the cost. That is not to say the cost is not high, but the prize of knowing and walking intimately with the God of the universe is worth it all.

<hr>

DAY 84

Jesus replied, "What is impossible with men is possible with God."

LUKE 18:27

BE careful that you do not grow too old in your mind. Choose the youthful path—the path of exuberance, hope, idealism, and the joy of defining each day as totally new and unknown. Each day, embrace the fresh young spirit of Christ within you (which is a great defense against attitudes that are judgmental and doubting).

Of course, what I am encouraging is no easy thing. It's hard to cling to idealism and be an "adult" at the same time. People will call you naïve or ignorant; they will accuse you of being in denial of life's gritty underbelly. But idealism is the fountain of youth, and those who hold to it remain young right up to the day they die. I suppose that is because idealism acts as a strong guardian of innocence.

Do not allow your innocence to be stolen away from you. Stay young, and never lose faith in your ideals.

DAY 85

Do not turn aside
from any of the commands
I give you today, to the right or to the left,
following other gods and serving them.
DEUTERONOMY 28:14

WE long to spend time with God but can't take time to study His Word. We long to worship but can't seem to focus on God's presence for more than a few minutes. We long to know Him but, in reality, we aren't even sure what that means in the busy context of daily life. The problem is that many of us are trying to serve God and an idol at the same time.

"What idol?" you may ask. "I don't serve any idol!" But let me explain what I mean. In our busy culture, we are all tempted to shape our lives around the "god" of "getting it all done"—all the projects, the prospects, the finances, the workouts, the relationships, you name it. We want to be productive. We want to feel successful. And everyone tells us that we must serve this "to-do list" god in order to be a "highly effective" person.

The problem with idols is that they promise things they can never deliver. If you want a life rich with meaning, serving the "to-do list" god will never get you there. Your efforts will be futile because your god will never be satisfied. No matter how hard you work, there will always be more to do. The list never ends.

The good news is this: You can let go of the "to-do list" burdens simply by changing your goal for each day. Instead of trying to "get it all done" today, make a commitment today to simply "be faithful." God, after all, did not call you to follow a list. He called you to follow a person.

DAY 86

You know when I sit and when I rise;
you perceive my thoughts from afar.
You discern my going out and my lying down;
you are familiar with all my ways.
Before a word is on my tongue you know it completely,
O LORD.

PSALM 139:2–4

WHENEVER you try to explain your heart to anyone—whether they be new friends or old ones—

you quickly realize what a difficult task it is to make your true self known. Even in the best of conditions, the people who want to love you will nonetheless misperceive you or misunderstand you. In some cases, they may even miss "seeing" you altogether.

Despite our best efforts, we each come to one another with a suitcase full of biases and presuppositions, stereotypes, and narrow perceptions. It's very hard for any of us to leave our own little world and enter fully into another's. The fact is that most of us are far too self-absorbed.

That is why I find my heart bursting with joy over the wonderful fact that God knows me so completely. It is marvelous to "be known" and, most especially, to be known by God. How thankful I am that I have no need to explain to Him every smirk or wince or chuckle or tear as they each come to my life. He knows it all completely—far better than I do, actually.

So as the breezes and storms of everyday life pass through you (and you through them), you do not need to explain the song those winds play on your soul. You need only glance at Him in the trees, or see His laughter in the clouds. . .and smile. He knows. Before a word is on your tongue, He knows. If that isn't peace, then I don't know what is.

As Jesus and his disciples were on their way, he came to a village where a woman named Martha opened her home to him. She had a sister called Mary, who sat at the Lord's feet listening to what he said. But Martha was distracted by all the preparations that had to be made. She came to him and asked, "Lord, don't you care that my sister has left me to do the work by myself? Tell her to help me!" "Martha, Martha," the Lord answered, "you are worried and upset about many things, but only one thing is needed. Mary has chosen what is better, and it will not be taken away from her."

LUKE 10:38–42

WHEN Jesus chided Martha for being distracted and worried about too many things, we are prone to agree with Him. After all, if we had the Lord of all creation and Savior of our souls sitting in our living rooms, chances are we wouldn't ignore Him in favor of doing our chores. No, we aren't like Martha at all, are we?

But Martha was not doing "busy work," she was doing things that really needed to be done. What's more, she was doing it for Jesus' benefit. That's right—she was making preparations for Jesus. Perhaps we are not so unlike Martha after all.

If Martha was doing "good stuff" for Jesus, why do you think He chided her for doing it? The answer is simple, though we often resist believing it. When Jesus said, "Only one thing is needed," He wasn't exaggerating. What is required to live a fulfilled and abundant life? The "one thing" that Mary was doing—sitting at Jesus' feet, gazing up at His face, and listening to His words.

This truth is profound and difficult for many of us to apply to our lives. You see, deep down we really want life to be about us—our ability to get stuff, our "good" works, our achievements for God. But life isn't about us, and it doesn't come from us. Life comes from Jesus—and nothing else.

Mary chose the better way. Will you?

DAY 88

What is more,
I consider everything a loss compared to the surpassing greatness of knowing Christ Jesus my Lord,
for whose sake I have lost all things.
I consider them rubbish, that I may gain Christ.
PHILIPPIANS 3:8

WHEN once you have really decided to abandon all for Christ, your role as an emissary servant for

Jesus becomes the sum of your identity and purpose in this world. And, therefore, you long for anything that lies outside that description to be cut away from your life.

This internal transformation of your values has a profound effect on all of your relationships—even on the way you look at relationships in general. For example, the single man who has made this choice begins to filter his relationships with women through his commitment to Jesus. The question in his heart is no longer, "Do I want to date this person?" or even "Do I want to get married someday?" Rather, the question becomes, "Would dating this person (or pursuing a wife at all) advance or hinder God's call on my life?" For the heart abandoned to Christ, life is about furthering God's kingdom above all else—even above our own desires for marriage and family.

You cannot claim to have abandoned all for Jesus and still hold some issues in reserve. God knows what you need far better than you ever will. If He wants you to be married, then He is perfectly capable of bringing you and your spouse together without any "help" from you. Therefore, abandon yourself to His care. Concern yourself with furthering His kingdom. And let Him concern Himself with the desires of your heart.

DAY 89

Then he got into the boat
and his disciples followed him.
Without warning, a furious storm came up
on the lake, so that the waves swept over the boat.
But Jesus was sleeping. The disciples went and woke
him, saying, "Lord, save us! We're going to drown!"
He replied, "You of little faith, why are you so
afraid?" Then he got up and rebuked the winds
and the waves, and it was completely calm.
MATTHEW 8:23–26

THERE will be times when you will face situations similar to the storm the disciples encountered. You will have followed Jesus into calm waters, and suddenly the rough, dangerous waters will threaten your life. Of course, you still know Jesus is with you. But He hasn't come to your rescue. He hasn't rushed in to calm your fears. As far as you can tell, it seems as though He is asleep in the boat.

When this happens (and it most certainly will), what will you do? When the first twelve disciples faced this peril, they panicked. Their faith crashed. They cried desperately for Jesus to wake up—feeling quite certain that if He didn't awaken, they would all perish in the storm.

But would they really have perished? Apparently, Jesus didn't think so. Once they awakened Him with their cries for help, did He rush to save them? Well, yes, He did perform a miracle by calming the storm. But that wasn't the first thing He did. First, He reprimanded His disciples for their lack of faith.

Does Jesus seem to be sleeping while you face danger? Before you panic, consider this: Perhaps the real danger you face is not your difficult circumstance but the possibility that you may not trust God.

DAY 90

In a large house there are articles not only of gold and silver, but also of wood and clay; some are for noble purposes and some for ignoble. If a man cleanses himself from the latter, he will be an instrument for noble purposes, made holy, useful to the Master and prepared to do any good work. Flee the evil desires of youth, and pursue righteousness, faith, love and peace, along with those who call on the Lord out of a pure heart.

2 TIMOTHY 2:20–22

THE word for "flee" in this passage is the Greek work *phuego*. It carries a sense of extreme urgency, as in a fugitive fleeing from his or her pursuing captors. The meaning of these verses is this: Once the Lord has set you free, you must run away as far as possible from the bondage that held you. For your old captors can pursue you and overtake you again if you become arrogant and let down your guard.

Never forget that the ground you have gained can be lost again. Satan is a thief; it is his nature to steal from your inheritance. And what binds the strong man so that the thief may enter? Many things, perhaps, but certainly chief among them is pride. "Pride goes before a fall," and whatever door Satan sneaks through, pride has been there first to undo the lock. So do not be arrogant, but run from the darkness to the light as an escaped prisoner running from death to life. For that is the truth of the matter.

DAY 91

One thing God has spoken,
two things have I heard:
that you, O God, are strong,
and that you, O Lord, are loving.
Surely you will reward each person
according to what he has done.
PSALM 62:11–12

WHEN your heart is filled with sorrow, it does no good to try to hide or deny how you feel. Your pain is real, and you have a right to feel it. Don't let anyone tell you differently. Like all feelings, sorrow is a tool in the Spirit's hand and can be used to sculpt your soul into something quite magnificent and pure. But God cannot use your pain if you bury it under layers of busyness and fakery.

So, then, when you are sorrowful, you must give yourself permission to feel. But be careful that you don't let sorrow overshadow your faith. Sorrow is not sin, but it often brings the temptation to sin—particularly with respect to your beliefs about God. There are two great lies that sorrow promotes: One, that God is not capable of helping you; and two, that God does not love you enough to help you. If you believe either of these lies, your faith will be shipwrecked, and your sorrow will overwhelm your soul.

Don't let this happen. When you are sorrowful, feel your sorrow. But in the midst of your pain, cling desperately to these truths: You, O God, are strong, and You, O Lord, are loving.

As long as you believe these two things, no sorrow can ever be too great to bear.

But he said to me,
"My grace is sufficient for you,
for my power is made perfect in weakness."
Therefore I will boast all the more gladly about my
weaknesses, so that Christ's power may rest on me.
That is why, for Christ's sake,
I delight in weaknesses, in insults, in hardships,
in persecutions, in difficulties.
For when I am weak, then I am strong.

2 CORINTHIANS 12:9–10

ONE of our greatest needs as Christians is to embrace and accept our own frailty. You and I need Jesus more desperately today than ever. But we are often too scared to look at the absolute weakness of our hearts. The sad truth is this: We are too proud and too frightened to admit our vulnerability. . .too broken in our souls to admit that we are utterly frail and desperately needy.

We give lip service to Jesus, but in our daily lives we often do not live as though we really need a Savior. Instead, we become adept at self-rescue and self-sufficiency—or rather, the illusion of these things. In truth, we are not really adept at self-sufficiency at all, because all of our attempts to take care of ourselves never work. But, even with this evidence, we tenaciously keep trying to save our own souls—over and over again—repeatedly clinging to the belief that we are strong despite all the evidence that we are not.

Do you believe you are a strong person? Then God's Word offers you this advice: Become weak, so that you may become strong. How wise that God has chosen to express His power through our weaknesses and not our strengths! That is why God's grace (that is, His power for life) comes freely to the humble, for the humble have no problem admitting their desperately needy condition.

The truth is this: You are vulnerable and frail. You are not strong. You cannot save yourself or keep yourself safe from harm. That is the truth about you apart from Christ. And if this offends you, then you are still believing lies.

DAY 93

Among the many nations there was no king like him. He was loved by his God, and God made him king over all Israel, but even he was led into sin by foreign women.
NEHEMIAH 13:26

EVEN Solomon blew it. What a letdown! Here he was, the wisest man ever to live outside of Christ, and in the end his own weakness still led him into self-destruction. Didn't he see it coming? We don't know. Maybe he thought he was wise enough to handle temptation. Or maybe he underestimated his own weakness as a person.

The raw truth of the matter is this: Your weaknesses can destroy you. They can dismantle all the good things you've worked to build in your life. They can rob you of all your joy and leave your soul bankrupt. And that's exactly what they will do, if you underestimate their potential for harm.

And don't think that your strengths can save you. "Well, yes, I have a problem with that, but surely there are enough good things in my heart to more than make up for it. I'll be all right." No, you won't. Solomon was extremely wise. God loved him and blessed him exceedingly. But wisdom is only effective when it is put into action. Solomon grew proud, and so he never confronted his weakness, a weakness that prompted him to go against his father's last words and God's direct commands. A weakness that caused division in his family and, eventually, in the kingdom he had worked so hard to build.

Therefore, be wary of that pet weakness you tend to excuse as unimportant. It's more important than you know. Accept your weaknesses—openly and without reservation. Present them humbly to God, knowing that where you are weak, He is strong. And then, show your weaknesses no mercy whatsoever.

*But when God,
who set me apart from birth and called me
by his grace, was pleased to reveal his Son in me
so that I might preach him among the Gentiles,
I did not consult any man.*

GALATIANS 1:15–16

GOD is not a "people pleaser." He never works within our timetables. Neither does He feel the slightest obligation to explain why He often, perhaps usually, makes us wait for things—even things that matter to us a great deal. He is God, and we are not. We simply have to accept that.

God does have a plan for our lives. But, much to the chagrin of many, His plan has little to do with making us comfortable. It also has little to do with making sure we understand everything that happens to us. Instead, God's plan has one objective—the revelation of His Son in the world.

Although God certainly loved Paul, God had a plan for him that went beyond Paul's own dreams and comforts. Paul understood that. He never said that God revealed his Son in him "so that he would have peace and safety," or "so that he would be financially successful," or "so that all of his questions would be answered." No, Paul said God had saved him "so that I might preach him among the Gentiles."

God's plan, not Paul's. And if it's God's plan, it naturally happens in God's timing.

God set apart Paul from birth, but He didn't reveal Himself to Paul until the Damascus road—after Paul's life had already been entrenched in lies for years, and after many Christians had already been killed as a direct result of the lies Paul believed. Have you ever wondered why God didn't step into Paul's life sooner? It doesn't make any sense. . .until you understand that God's plan didn't guarantee Paul a perfect life; it did guarantee the revelation of Jesus.

What is God's plan for you? It's to reveal His Son through your life. Make your vision of God's plan any smaller than that, and you will never be able to accept with joy the things God allows to happen in your life.

DAY 95

My God, my God,
why have you forsaken me? Why are you so
far from saving me, so far from the words of
my groaning? O my God, I cry out by day,
but you do not answer, by night, and am not silent.
PSALM 22:1–2

SOMETIMES your spiritual life is stagnant. Or, at least, all the evidence points to this conclusion.

You want to know Christ more deeply; you may even long to know Him. Your soul may ache with hunger for a deeper revelation of His presence in your life. And so you read devotional books, do Bible studies, go on mission trips, or serve in the church in some capacity. But your spiritual life remains unmoved. You wonder what is wrong with you. You wonder why God is silent.

When these times come (and they come to us all), the important thing is that you remain connected to your heart. Don't let go of God—of your longing to know God—no matter how painful the seeking becomes. You may think your efforts are fruitless, but they are not.

You must understand that the very longing you possess is God's gift—a gift that is doing a work of transformation deep within your soul. In fact, the longing itself is the presence of the Holy Spirit in your heart. Be assured that God will answer your cry for a deeper knowledge of Him. But first the cry itself must complete its work in your life. Allow that to happen, and when you sense His presence at last, you will find yourself changed in a way you hadn't expected. You will be sanctified, ready to receive Him in new ways. And you will immediately realize that, had He come any earlier, you would not have been able to receive Him at all.

DAY 96

So God created
man in his own image,
in the image of God he created him;
male and female he created them.
GENESIS 1:27

SACREDNESS is locked up within your human personality—a holy aspect that is as much a part of you as are your eyes or your hair. Even though you are fallen, even though you sin, you still bear a sacred image or "reflection" of God within your body and your soul. This image is made all the more sacred because it is unique. You reflect God's image in a particular way that no one else, in times past or present, could ever duplicate. And once you are gone, that unique reflection of God will die with you. No one will ever be able to recreate it again.

Of course, on some level we all recognize this sacredness about ourselves. It's what tells us that every life is precious, that no one should be treated unjustly, that every soul deserves respect. Though we see the sacredness of life in others, we often struggle most to believe this sacredness resides within our own hearts as well. For though we are sacred, we are also fallen. And we've spent years watching ourselves treat others in horrible ways, and we've felt the sting of being repeatedly treated as less than sacred ourselves. Over time we convince our hearts that we are not so special after all.

This is a lie. Despite the Fall, despite the sins you have committed, despite the sins committed against you, something sacred in you remains, something beautiful, something worthy of honor and respect. Something, perhaps, even worthy of awe. This something is your unique reflection of God.

Therefore, no matter how many people misunderstand you or attack you or ignore you or criticize you, you must always make the choice to revel in being yourself. To do anything less would be to deny the sacredness of your soul. And it would deny the world a reflection of God that it can see in no other way.

DAY 97

*"Therefore I tell you,
do not worry about your life, what you will eat
or drink; or about your body, what you will wear.
Is not life more important than food,
and the body more important than clothes?"*
MATTHEW 6:25

DOESN'T it seem strange that Jesus would command us to do something that at once seems not only impractical, but even impossible to obey? "How can I give no thought to what I will eat or drink?

Should I expect my food and drink to magically appear on my table every meal? What about my bills? My clothing? My shelter? If I don't see to these things, who will?"

But the command does not say to ignore or give no thought to these basic needs of life; it says not to worry about them. More precisely, it commands us not to take on anxiety about them. Now Jesus' words take on a much more reasonable aspect. Yes, you should work hard. You should do all you can to provide for your needs. You should be a good steward of your resources. But in the midst of all this, you should not fall into worry about any of it.

"What's wrong with worrying about things sometimes?" some might ask. "Isn't that just part of being human?" No, it's part of being sinful, separated from God. Worry always stems from fear—fear that our needs will not be met, fear that someone will steal what we have, fear that we will not be successful in this endeavor or that. This sort of fear can never coexist with faith. Faith says, "I will obey God. I will do my best at all times. I never need to worry about anything. Instead, I will trust God and enjoy my life."

Worry is sin. Never allow yourself to be lulled into thinking it is anything more acceptable than that.

Flee from sexual immorality.
All other sins a man commits are outside his body,
but he who sins sexually sins against his own body.
Do you not know that your body is
a temple of the Holy Spirit, who is in you,
whom you have received from God.
You are not your own; you were bought at a price.
Therefore honor God with your body.

1 CORINTHIANS 6:18–20

THAT you should commit yourself to sexual purity is obvious. The trick comes in figuring out what exactly that means for you. The command is, after all, somewhat gray. Should I avoid all contact with the opposite sex before marriage? Is that sexual purity? Or should I just avoid "technical" sexual relations? What about flirting? Making out? Spending lots of time alone with a member of the opposite sex? Can I do those things and still be sexually pure?

Well, maybe. Or maybe not. Admittedly, it would be much easier if God had made His command for sexual purity more black and white. Why did God make this important command so seemingly vague? Out of respect for us, really, because He knows we are not clones of one another. We are individuals, with individual strengths and weaknesses and, therefore, individual limits to what we can do and remain sexually pure in our hearts.

It is tragic that so many Christians use this perceived vagueness as a loophole to do what they want sexually. "If the Bible doesn't overtly say I can't do something, then I guess it means I can." Such an attitude is not right and completely misses the point of the command. The goal is to "flee from sexual immorality," not "see what you can get away with and still technically remain a virgin." Sexual purity begins in your heart. Make that your focus, your goal, your passion in following Christ.

DAY 99

After the earthquake came a fire,
but the LORD was not in the fire.
And after the fire came a gentle whisper.
1 KINGS 19:12

GOD rarely speaks to us in ways that are overbearing or obvious, but in ways that can be easily misunderstood. He speaks most often in a gentle whisper that forces us to stop and pay attention. "Was that God speaking," we ask ourselves, "or was it just my head?" Determining which is the case takes prayer— and more careful listening. But God whispers in everything that touches our lives. Sadly, we're often too preoccupied to hear it or, even worse, too savvy to accept it as anything more than circumstance.

God is speaking; it is we who must learn how to listen. Too often, we cry to God for bold signs from heaven—a voice of thunder accompanied by the appearance of angels or something equally loud and flashy. But all the while God is speaking in myriad ways around us, and we miss His messages entirely.

Once we begin the discipline of constantly saying from the heart, "Speak, Lord, for Your servant is listening," life will take on new color and depth. Every day becomes a romance. The more we choose to be still and listen—and believe—the more we will be able to hear His voice. At the same time, we will realize that we never really needed the flashy signs from heaven after all. We needed only to believe.

DAY 100

For Christ's love compels us,
because we are convinced that one died for all,
and therefore all died.
2 CORINTHIANS 5:14

THE word for "compel" in this passage means "to be forced as a prisoner." Paul is saying that he has been taken prisoner by God's love, and that love now compels him to move in a particular direction.

You can always recognize people who have been taken prisoner by God's love. They move through life differently from the rest of humanity; they stand out in bright colors against the common backdrop of gray. They are joyful folk—unruffled, unrushed, uncontrolled by the common pressures of life. Their countenance is obviously filled with the Holy Spirit.

It's not that they have a monopoly on the Holy Spirit; it's that the Holy Spirit has a monopoly on them. They are captive to Him—meaning that they are continually captivated by Him, above everything else.

The gateway to encountering God's love in this way is simple faith. And once you allow yourself to be captured, life becomes beautifully simple. Your every motivation stems from love—love is what lies before you, and love is what follows behind. You are caught in its flow. And love is what compels you toward accomplishing God's will.

Get in the habit of praying each day for God's love to capture your heart. Then take time to let yourself be captivated by the demonstrations of God's love all around you. He is loving you all the time.

Whatever happens, conduct yourselves in a manner worthy of the gospel of Christ. . . .
PHILIPPIANS 1:27

THE gospel of Christ is a treasure more costly and more lovely than the most priceless jewel on earth. It is more precious than any personal goals or loves or struggles or fears. It is more valuable, in fact, than our human lives—as attested by the thousands of Christian martyrs who have died for the sake of the gospel. And this is the gospel that resides in your heart.

It seems strange, then, when Christians go around acting as if they possess no treasure at all. We are God's ambassadors, carrying within our hearts the most expensive gift He could offer to the world. Given this fact, Paul's instruction seems obvious. "Whatever happens," we should carry the gospel within our breast with reverence and humility. But more often we choose to be full of ourselves instead of the gospel.

"It's just that my girlfriend and I had this fight. . ."

"It's just that I've had a lot of pressure from work. . ."

"It's just that I didn't get enough sleep last night. . ."

It's amazing how petty our reasons are for tossing our responsibility to conduct ourselves in a manner worthy of the gospel of Christ. Remember, you are not your own now; you were bought at a price—Christ's life. Therefore, honor God. . .

Whatever happens.

DAY 102

Do you not know?
Have you not heard?
The LORD is the everlasting God,
the Creator of the ends of the earth.
He will not grow tired or weary. . . .
ISAIAH 40:28

EVERYONE, however spiritually or emotionally balanced he or she claims to be, gets exhausted spiritually at times. When you find yourself exhausted physically, you know exactly what you need to recover. Rest. Food. Sleep. But when you find yourself exhausted emotionally or spiritually, where do you turn? How do you recover from that sort of exhaustion?

The first key to recovery is to accept the fact that you are exhausted and to recognize it as a normal and expected part of life. Imagine a woman is running in a marathon. When she finishes the race, she is, naturally, quite exhausted. But she doesn't get mad at herself for being tired, does she? Of course not. Yet that is exactly what we are prone to do to ourselves when we become exhausted in spirit. "What's wrong with me? Why can't I serve with the same passion as I did last year?" Nothing is wrong with you. You are emotionally and spiritually wiped out, that's all. It happens to all of us. Accept it.

The second key to your emotional and spiritual recovery is to recognize from where your strength comes. "The Lord. . .will not grow tired or weary. . ." This is one of the ways God is wholly different from you, and you should be overjoyed by the fact. He does not grow tired like a human being does; He is always bursting with energy. So when you feel spent, you can drag your weary heart into His embrace. His strength is sufficient for both of you. He can carry your load and replenish your soul at the same time. And it doesn't tax Him in the least.

DAY 103

"The poor and needy search for water,
but there is none;
their tongues are parched with thirst.
But I the LORD will answer them;
I, the God of Israel, will not forsake them.
I will make rivers flow on barren heights, and springs
within the valleys. I will turn the desert into pools
of water, and the parched ground into springs.
I will put in the desert the cedar and the acacia,
the myrtle and the olive. I will set pines in
the wasteland, the fir and the cypress together,
so that people may see and know, may consider and
understand, that the hand of the LORD has done this,
that the Holy One of Israel has created it."
ISAIAH 41:17–20

ONCE you begin reading through the Old Testament, one theme becomes abundantly clear: God loves deserts. Or, at the very least, He loves to use them for His purposes a great deal of the time.

"But why does God love desert places?" you may ask. I suspect the answer is this: God loves deserts because He loves redemption. In other words, He loves to redeem things; He loves to take things that are broken or dead and fill them with beauty and life. So He doesn't love the desert for the desert's sake; He loves it because it's the best place for Him to show His power to redeem. "I will turn the desert into pools of water, and the parched ground into springs. . . ."

The Israelites wandered in physical deserts. We most often wander in deserts of the heart. But God uses our deserts for the same reasons—to expose our desperate need for Him and to reveal His power to save. "so that people may see and know, may consider and understand, that the hand of the Lord has done this."

Deserts are where God reveals Himself to us. That is what makes them lovely. Once we come to see our deserts in this light, then they become beautiful to us, as well. Are you in a desert—in your job, perhaps? In your relationships? In your quest to know God? Then don't lose heart, but let your thirst drive you to God. He is right now in the process of redeeming you.

DAY 104

You will keep in perfect peace him whose mind is steadfast, because he trusts in you.
ISAIAH 26:3

A better rendering of this verse might be, "You will keep in perfect peace him whose mind is at rest because his confidence is in you." Peace will never come to us until we first learn to rest our minds in

God; we need to stop trying to figure everything out for ourselves. You don't have to always understand what God is doing before you trust Him; it is enough that God understands. He knows what He is doing, and He has never once asked you to spend all your mental energy trying to dissect His plan. He asks only that you trust Him and rest in His goodness. Once you do that, His peace becomes your constant companion, immediately flooding every aspect of your life.

But you say, "It's not that I don't trust Him. I just want to understand what's going on." The longing for understanding is not a bad thing, but be certain that your longing doesn't reflect a misplaced confidence. Sometimes we want to understand not because we trust in God, but precisely because we don't. We "long to understand" so we can check up on God and make sure He's handling the affairs of our lives in a reasonable way—a way that seems right to our own minds.

Is your confidence in God, or in your own human reasoning? Rest your mind in God. Stop trying to figure everything out for yourself. Only then will you know His peace.

*If it is possible, as far as it depends on you,
live at peace with everyone.*

ROMANS 12:18

SOMETIMES it is not possible to live at peace
with everyone. You can do everything you know to
love others well; you can try to understand their motives and their actions; you can listen intently to their
concerns; you can change your approach and your
priorities to accommodate their preferences. And,
after all your efforts, you still find that you cannot live
at peace with them. Or they cannot live at peace with
you. Sometimes it just doesn't work out.

Relationships are like bridges between two
hearts. It takes a commitment from both parties to
bridge the gap between you. And when a breakdown
occurs, there is a limit to what one person can do to
repair the damage. You should, of course, do all that
you can to repair the breach, but always be careful to
recognize the limit of what you can do. If you have
sinned, repent. If you have broken trust, commit
yourself to make it right. But, having done all this, if
the other person won't forgive you, or refuses to trust
again, then you must be willing to let go.

The great temptation in broken relationships is
to take responsibility for another person's conclusions
about you. No one else controls what you think, or

how you feel, do they? The same is true for those around you. After you have done all you can to make peace, you have to give others space to draw their own conclusions. And if they decide they cannot live in peace with you, then you must walk away—even when you know their conclusions about you are wrong.

The most important thing, then, is that you always make it your ambition to love everyone in a way that honors Christ. In the end, what others conclude about you is out of your control.

DAY 106

*But even if I am being poured
out like a drink offering on the sacrifice
and service coming from your faith,
I am glad and rejoice with all of you.*
PHILIPPIANS 2:17

ARE you glad when you are called to sacrifice your rights for the sake of another person? Does the prospect of being a "drink offering" for someone else's life fill you with joy? There are times when God calls us to lay aside our own desires, preferences, and needs for the sake of another person's faith. When God lays this command on you, be careful not only to obey, but to obey joyfully. It is a joyful thing to lay down your life for another person—ask any parent. But it is also a selfless thing; and that is something our sinful nature abhors. So you must consciously revel in the joy of watching another benefit from your sacrifice. You must keep yourself in joy, for the instant you entertain a selfish thought, resentment will come in like a flood.

God places in all of our lives individuals who are inherently difficult to love. They are selfish people, usually. Or foolish, ignorant folk. Or arrogant types who don't even know you exist until they need an audience to admire them. And, even though these folks do not know how to love in a manner worthy of Christ, God nevertheless calls you to simply love them. You are God's secret weapon in their lives. Your love is having an impact on their selfish ways; it's reshaping them, provoking them to consider their lives before God. You, of course, may never see the fruits of your sacrifice on their behalf. But that is not the important thing anyway. The important thing is that you sacrifice with joy. As long as you do this, God will always bring you into a place of abundance in the end.

DAY 107

*Simon answered, "Master,
we've worked hard all night and haven't caught
anything. But because you say so, I will let down
the nets." When they had done so, they caught such a
large number of fish that their nets began to break.*
LUKE 5:5–6

IT isn't enough just to do the right thing, or the thing that's logical and prudent. You have to do that thing when God tells you to do it, and not before or after. You may know the right thing to do, but if you don't wait for God's timing, you will only wear yourself out and accomplish absolutely nothing. God's timing is impeccable; He knows exactly when that next step needs to be taken. And He will tell you, if you will just wait for Him.

But, more often than not, that is not our way. We are more like the disciples, who encountered Jesus with a whiny disposition. "For heaven's sake, Jesus, I've been trying to do this for years, and it has never worked like it's supposed to. And now you're telling me to do it again? Well, okay, but I think this is a waste of time."

In reality, though, time was only wasted before you received God's direction. When the things you are doing are God-driven, the results will be obvious. Think about the disciples' fishing nets, so full they began to burst. God always supports what He initiates. But He will never support our attempts to do the right thing outside of His power and love.

Don't get ahead of God. It's a total waste of both your time and His. Instead, discipline yourself to wait for God's word. The Word, after all, is what provides the power to accomplish anything at all. If you doubt that, then you need to reread the book of Genesis. "God said. . .and there was. . . ."

DAY 108

"Leave her alone,"
said Jesus. "Why are you bothering her?
She has done a beautiful thing to me."
MARK 14:6

HAVE you really understood that you can do things for God that He finds beautiful? Have you considered that you can bring gifts to God? The woman's love for Jesus compelled her to find a way to lavish Him with love tokens. Her demonstration of love was creative. It was sacrificial. It was humbling. And it was something Jesus could never have done for Himself.

God cannot give Himself your love. He cannot give Himself your praise, or your devotion, or your resources. These (and many others like them) are gifts of love that only you can give to Him. They are the tools of divine romance. Have you ever realized that you can move the heart of God with a simple song?

Do you want a more intimate relationship with God? Then cultivate one. Lavish God with the private gifts that move Him. Be creative. This week, do "a beautiful thing" for Him. Next week, do another. Before long, you will have all the romance with God that you ever dreamed.

DAY 109

"Just as the Son of Man did not come to be served, but to serve. . ."
MATTHEW 20:28

THE call of every Christian is the same in principle as the call of Christ Himself. We are called so that we might serve, not so that we might be served. For this reason, the end goal of every Christian should be to lay down his or her life as a sacrifice in service of others. If that is not our ultimate aim, then we will have missed the point of the gospel entirely.

But before we can serve others well, we must allow Christ to serve us.

When we come to Christ, our souls are in a horrific mess. Our minds are filled with garbage from the past; our wounded hearts reek with the stench of bitterness and pride. More than anything, we need to be loved and healed. We need to be made whole. And, in the life of every new Christian, this is precisely what the Holy Spirit sets out to do.

Too often, though, we fight God on this point; we turn away from His offers of love because we don't feel like we deserve such lavish attention—especially without paying a price for it. But we must lay down our self-concepts, our pride, and our shame. Letting ourselves be loved by Jesus is the first essential step toward becoming a servant. Until we learn to receive God's love, we will never be able to give it away. After all, we cannot give what we do not possess.

There will come a time when God will call you to lay down your life in sacrifice to others. He does not want you to lay down your life because you think you are worthless or less valuable than others. He wants you to lay down your life because you desperately want others to experience the same love that has made you whole.

DAY 110

*When the people saw the thunder
and lightning and heard the trumpet and saw
the mountain in smoke, they trembled with fear.
They stayed at a distance and said to Moses,
"Speak to us yourself and we will listen.
But do not have God speak to us or we will die."*

EXODUS 20:18–19

THE Christian life is a great deal easier as long as God does not speak to us directly. As long as He does not speak specifically to us, we have no imperative for our lives—no specific vision, no unique command. We are free to deal with Christ on the level of common sense. We can live sensibly, do sensible things. Nothing out of the ordinary, really. Nothing extreme. And for many Christians, this is their preferred way of living. They really don't want anything more.

"Speak to us yourself and we will listen. But do not have God speak to us or we will die." We are often just like the Israelites on this point. We don't want God to speak to us directly, because we do not want to die to our own ways. We know inherently that once we allow God close enough to speak to us, we will be forced to deal with Him at the point of obedience. We can no longer remain in the realm of "fuzzy" Christianity—it's either "obey," or "disobey." But as long as we hear only God's servant—a pastor, for example—then we always have a way to weasel out of the command. We're free to say, "Well, that's just your interpretation of God's Word. I'm not sure that would be a sensible thing for me to do just now."

If you hear God's voice, you have to give up living by what sounds sensible. God's commands rarely seem sensible to our human way of thinking, but they always lead us to abundant life. Are you running from God's voice because you do not want to die? "For whoever wants to save his life will lose it, but whoever loses his life for me will find it" (Matthew 16:25).

DAY 111

"Sir," the woman said,
"you have nothing to draw with and the well
is deep. Where can you get this living water?
Are you greater than our father Jacob, who gave
us the well and drank from it himself, as did also
his sons and his flocks and herds?" Jesus answered,
"Everyone who drinks this water will be thirsty again,
but whoever drinks the water I give him will never
thirst. Indeed, the water I give him will become
in him a spring of water welling up to eternal life."
JOHN 4:11–14

NOTICE that Jesus never answers the woman's

question. That's because it's the wrong question. Her question is borne out of human reasoning, not from faith. And God rarely answers us along the line of our human reasoning, because He knows that human reason almost always leads us to a dead end in matters of faith.

Many times when we think God doesn't answer us, it is because we are asking Him the wrong question. "How will you provide for this need?" "Where is the wife (or husband) I long for?" "When will I have a job with a decent salary?" All of these questions stem from our human reasoning. They are not usually borne from faith. And God is not likely to answer them.

When God is silent to your questions, be quick to lay them aside. Don't cling to them tenaciously in your arrogance. "I cannot believe," you say, "until I understand this point." Yes, you can. If you truly needed that particular question answered, then God would have answered it long ago. Chances are that God is trying to tell you something you do need to know, but you stopped listening because you are stuck thinking about the question He won't answer. If the woman at the well had clung to her question, she would have never heard the more important truth that Jesus was sharing—that He had living water to offer her. In the end, where He got it hardly mattered. What mattered was that He was offering it to her.

Don't miss the gift of God for the sake of your stubbornness.

Remember this:
Whoever sows sparingly will also reap sparingly,
and whoever sows generously will also reap generously.
Each man should give what he has decided in his
heart to give, not reluctantly or under compulsion,
for God loves a cheerful giver. And God is able
to make all grace abound to you, so that in all
things at all times, having all that you need,
you will abound in every good work.

2 CORINTHIANS 9:6–8

THESE verses should always be taken as a whole. That is, the second principle is dependent on the first. We should not expect God to make all grace abound to us if we are sowing sparingly. We should not expect that God will provide all that we need if we are not generous with what we already have. God's grace and provisions flow through a web of relationships. We can dam the blessings of God by our selfishness. If we don't allow His blessings to flow freely through us to others, then they will eventually cease to flow into our lives at all.

"But I can't just give everything away, can I?" you may ask. "Being a good steward means giving within my means." No, being a good steward means giving as the owner of the goods has instructed. The blessings you have are not yours to possess; they are the

Lord's. And God has instructed us to give generously, to sow generously, to take risks in giving.

God will at times call you to give beyond your means. Not because He wants you to be in need, but because He wants to deepen the reservoir of His grace in your life. As long as we place our trust in our physical provisions, God's grace remains merely academic. But once we begin to give generously, beyond the line of what is "safe," then the grace of God comes alive in ways we had never imagined. "From the fullness of his grace we have all received one blessing after another" (John 1:16).

DAY 113

You are still worldly.
For since there is jealousy and
quarreling among you, are you not worldly?
Are you not acting like mere men?
1 CORINTHIANS 3:3

JESUS is constantly saying to us, "Come up higher." Our vision of Christ's salvation is too small; our understanding of its effects are far too ordinary and mundane. We thank God for the grace to "make it through the day," and we do not begin to see that God's grace has done far more than that. His grace has transformed us from the inside out, so that we are no longer "mere" men and women. We have been reborn into an entirely new race of people. We were born as sons and daughters of Adam, but through the blood of Christ we are now the sons and daughters of God. We are more than mere humans; we are more than conquerors.

Tragically, when Christians live as though they have not been changed at all. "For since there is jealousy and quarreling among you, are you not worldly?" To be jealous and quarrelsome is "only human." But no son or daughter of God has any reason to be petty or jealous of others, right? Unless perhaps these sons and daughters have forgotten that they are the inheritors of everything beautiful, everything glorious, everything pure and lovely that belongs to Christ. Yes, I suppose we could fall into pettiness and jealousy if we forget about that. But what a ridiculously huge thing to forget! We are co-heirs with Christ. As the heirs of God, we are called to live by a different standard now—a standard set and maintained by God's strength and holiness flowing through us.

Are you living in your human strength, or in God's? Living in our own strength, we will always come across as merely human to the world. But once we plug into God's grace, our lives take on a supernatural flow.

Come up higher.

DAY 114

When Jesus rose
early on the first day of the week,
he appeared first to Mary Magdalene,
out of whom he had driven seven demons.
She went and told those who had been with him
and who were mourning and weeping.
When they heard that Jesus was alive
and that she had seen him, they did not believe it.
Afterward Jesus appeared in a different form to
two of them while they were walking in the country.
These returned and reported it to the rest;
but they did not believe them either.
Later Jesus appeared to the Eleven as they were
eating; he rebuked them for their lack of faith
and their stubborn refusal to believe those
who had seen him after he had risen.
MARK 16:9–14

DON'T be quick to discount another person's testimony about Christ, just because it doesn't match up with the way Jesus has dealt with you. Salvation is the same for everyone, but the relationship with God that follows salvation is a uniquely personal thing. Jesus deals with each of us on an individual basis, and His approach will naturally differ from person to person. Therefore, be careful not to fall into the trap of making comparisons. This will only lead you to pass judgment on someone else's relationship with God. Or else to pass judgment on your own.

"Afterward Jesus appeared in a different form. . ." Don't be surprised when Jesus appears to someone else in a way that's totally foreign to your experience. Christ comes in many different forms, and nowhere is it written that you will know them all. So be very slow to say that someone's experience of Christ is false because it comes in a form that is unfamiliar to you. Instead, watch the fruit, and that will tell you whether the experience was genuine.

The real Jesus is far larger than we expect. He is perfectly willing to shatter the quaint theological borders we draw around Him.

DAY 115

At my first defense,
no one came to my support,
but everyone deserted me. . . . But the Lord
stood at my side and gave me strength. . . .
2 TIMOTHY 4:16–17

AT some point in life, every Christian must face the desert of desertion. This is the desert where you will be attacked by enemies who are too strong for you. And when you look around for help from your friends, you will find no one there. Jesus' friends truly loved Him, and yet they still deserted Him out of fear and ignorance. At some point, so will yours.

When the desert of desertion first comes, we are dumbfounded. "How could this have happened to me?" we wonder. But before long we realize that this abandonment had to take place—or we would never learn to lean fully on the One who will never leave us or forsake us.

"But the Lord stood at my side and gave me strength. . . ." We never truly discover that God's strength is all we need until His strength is all that we have. As long as we have other means of support, we will always tend to rely on them to the exclusion of God. The desert of desertion is essential, for only there can we learn the awesome security of building our identity and our security on the One who knows us truly, and who will always remain by our sides.

Do you feel alone or abandoned just now in your circumstances? Then stop thinking about the person or situation that has caused you to feel deserted. Instead, fix your eyes on Jesus. His love will not fail.

Nevertheless, each one should retain the place in life that the Lord assigned to him and to which God has called him. . . .

1 CORINTHIANS 7:17

ARE you content with the place in life to which God has you currently assigned? Or is your heart caught up in coveting the thing that God has not yet brought? More money? A different job? A spouse?

Admittedly, it is especially difficult for singles to remain content in their singleness, because everything in their environment tells them they should not be content. This is especially true of the current Christian culture in the West, which exalts marriage as the better and even more mature Christian path. What single person hasn't had well-meaning friends or family members try to "rescue" him or her from singleness—as though it were a prison to be escaped. Their intentions may be good, but their perspectives are far from biblical.

In the face of these cultural prejudices, as singles we must be all the more determined to remain content where God has placed us. God's timing is always perfect. He cannot be wrong. And so our singleness is not the result of some cosmic mistake that God has made. Nor is it the result of our lack of maturity, any more than our getting married would automatically mean we are mature. It is simply the place to which God has called us. And as long as He keeps us here, our focus should be to serve Him wholeheartedly from this place—as a single person.

While you are single, embrace your singleness as a gift and a calling. Cultivate contentment in being single—no matter how often the world tells you to do otherwise. This is not an abdication of your desire to be married; it is your proclamation of trust in God.

DAY 117

Jesus answered: "Don't you know me, Philip, even after I have been among you such a long time?"
JOHN 14:9

HOW long do we have to be around Jesus before we really know Him? The answer depends entirely on us. Sadly, some people can live around Jesus for years and never actually come to know Him at all. Perhaps they love the sense of His presence. Or they are charmed with His gifts. But they are not really interested in discovering Him. The real Jesus is far less palatable than their sweet fantasies about Him. God is, after all, as C. S. Lewis puts it in his Narnia tales, "not a tame Lion." In other words, He is too wild and wonderful and enormous for us to ever put into any small, safe box.

The question Jesus asked Philip no doubt cut him to the quick, and it should do the same for us. How long has Jesus loved you, pursued you, walked with you—and still you must admit you do not know Him? Jesus will always remain unknowable to us as long as we cling to our false ideas about Him. But once we make up our minds to lay aside our agendas and our endless lists of requests and simply seek Him—with no aim other than to know Him as He truly is—then the veil is torn away, and we find that Jesus has been standing right there all the time.

When we open our hearts to know Him truly, the first thing Jesus does is come in and shatter every fantasy we have concerning Him. This action on Christ's part can leave us disillusioned. "Why is Christ offending me so? This does not feel like love! Jesus is not who I expected at all."

But it is love, precisely because He is nothing like you expected. He is much more—and that is what He wants you to see.

DAY 118

Preach the Word;
be prepared in season and out of season;
correct, rebuke and encourage—
with great patience and careful instruction.
2 TIMOTHY 4:2

"IN season and out of season. . ." The season Paul speaks of may refer to circumstances. We are called to share the good news of Jesus:

- when we feel inspired—and when we don't;
- when we feel strong—and when we don't;
- when we see an opportunity coming—and when we don't;
- when we feel like caring—and when we don't.

One of the most dangerous attitudes Christians can adopt is one of "mandatory inspiration." They won't do anything by way of service to God unless they feel the very hand of God pressing them to act. But real love is a free choice, and most of the opportunities to love that God brings our way don't come by force. Rather, they come gently and quietly, and they can be easily ignored—so that we must choose them of our own free will.

The real ministry of God is not powered by inspiration but by compassion. "When Jesus landed and saw a large crowd, he had compassion on them and healed their sick" (Matthew 14:14); notice that the Gospel doesn't tell us if Jesus felt inspired or motivated to heal. In fact, He may have been tired and longing for some time alone. But He did not permit His tiredness or any other emotion to get in the way of His compassion.

Stop waiting for visions from heaven to tell you what to do. Instead, develop a heart of compassion for the world around you.

DAY 119

When the two disciples heard him say this, they followed Jesus. Turning around, Jesus saw them following and asked, "What do you want?" They said, "Rabbi" (which means Teacher), "where are you staying?" "Come," he replied, "and you will see."
JOHN 1:37–39

THE cry of our hearts is much like that of these two disciples. "I want to go where Jesus is!" But then we find out where Jesus has actually gone, and we are suddenly not so eager to follow Him. He goes to places we do not expect, even though they are the sort of places He has always gone—to the sick and the sinning.

Jesus likes to hang out with sinners. This comes as a shock to many Christians, so much so that they choose to put the fact out of their minds. "I could never go to that bar," the "good" Christian says. "What would it say about my faith?" What indeed! Jesus is already in that bar. . .or that prison. . .or that hospital. . .or that broken home. And He is waiting for you to join Him there.

Do you want to go where Jesus is? Then find the place where broken people gather, and you will find Him there with them. "It is not the healthy who need a doctor, but the sick" (Matthew 9:12).

DAY 120

Another disciple said to him,
"Lord, first let me go and bury my father."
But Jesus told him, "Follow me,
and let the dead bury their own dead."
MATTHEW 8:21–22

THERE will come a point in your Christian walk when you realize that your obedience to God is going to cost the people around you more than you thought. Once you have set your heart to obey, you rarely fall away from God's directive because of intentional rebellion against the Holy Spirit, but rather because of sympathy for other people's desires. For instance: "I know God is telling me to write this book, but those close to me feel hurt when I don't spend much time with them." It's true that they may be hurt, but that does not excuse you from obeying God.

"But I have responsibilities," you might say. "I can't just up and do this thing God commands without also considering all my other duties." What are the real responsibilities that God has given you, the ones we've discussed earlier in this book? These are the only duties with which you need to concern yourself. God never gives conflicting commands. Too often many of the "duties" to which we feel bound are not God-given at all, but rather things other people put on us, or merely things we put on ourselves to help us feel like we're in control.

God never commands us to do more than we can handle, but His commands generally come at a cost—both to us and to the people He has placed in our lives.

DAY 121

We are hard pressed on every side,
but not crushed; perplexed, but not in despair;
persecuted, but not abandoned;
struck down, but not destroyed.
We always carry around in our body
the death of Jesus, so that the life
of Jesus may also be revealed in our body.
2 CORINTHIANS 4:8–10

WE don't learn to endure hardship by developing a love for pain and suffering, but rather by learning to delight in seeing Christ manifested in us. In whatever circumstance or state you find yourself, the reason for life becomes the manifestation of Christ, "that the life of Jesus may also be revealed."

This very attitude, in fact, is what prevents us from feeling "crushed," "in despair," "abandoned," or "destroyed" in the midst of suffering. For every pain, however difficult, has at least this one purpose, which we can understand and hang our hat on: "that the life of Jesus may also be revealed in our body." Make this your ambition, and all the anxiety you feel because of the pain suddenly becomes channeled toward this single goal: "If I do nothing else through this, I will take delight in letting Jesus' light shine through me. I will make my pain an offering to Him to use as He will."

There is a beauty that comes to suffering, and it always comes along the line of self-forgetfulness. Once we forget ourselves, then even our pain ceases to be about us. Instead, it is about the manifestation of Jesus.

DAY 122

For it is commendable if a man bears up under the pain of unjust suffering because he is conscious of God. But how is it to your credit if you receive a beating for doing wrong and endure it? But if you suffer for doing good and you endure it, this is commendable before God. To this you were called, because Christ suffered for you, leaving you an example, that you should follow in his steps.

1 PETER 2:19–21

WHENEVER we are treated harshly or unjustly by others, our sense of justice is immediately outraged. "How dare he do that to me!" "Who does she think she is anyway?" But no sooner do we plan our counterattack than we find the Holy Spirit coming alongside us encouraging us to do nothing at all. And this, of course, makes absolutely no sense to us whatsoever.

"Why should I stand silent when someone mis-treats me? That's self-abusive! I can't just let some-one hurl insults at me and not defend myself." Of course you can. And there are times when you should, "because you are conscious of God."

We don't endure unjust suffering because we are spiritual wimps or because we are afraid to make a stand. We endure because we are conscious of God's place in our lives. We have entrusted ourselves to Him. He is our King; thus we trust that He will act on our behalf. "When they hurled their insults at him, he did not retaliate; when he suffered, he made no threats. Instead, he entrusted himself to him who judges justly" (1 Peter 2:23).

We cannot retaliate against those who attack us unless we first put God out of our minds. As long as He remains enthroned in us, as long as our trust is in Him, we will not feel the need to strike back at any attacker (though we certainly may still feel the urge). Our faith in God releases us from the need to defend ourselves. He has become our defense. "Do not take revenge, my friends, but leave room for God's wrath, for it is written: 'It is mine to avenge; I will repay,' says the Lord" (Romans 12:19).

*You prepare a table before me
in the presence of my enemies.
You anoint my head with oil; my cup overflows.*

PSALM 23:5

RARELY does God deliver us from the presence of our enemies. Instead, He delivers us right in front of them. He prepares a place of deliverance and celebration around us that our enemies cannot breach. They can still see us; they can even continue to hurl their spears at our hearts. But their attacks no longer reach us. For God is now standing between them and us.

When an enemy attacks, do not beg the Lord to remove your enemy or to remove you from their sight. Instead, ask Him to deliver you right in front of them. Once you do, He will come in and prepare a banquet table for you—right there before those who mean to harm you.

There is no safer place than to be seated at the banquet table of the King of the universe. At His table, His love surrounds you, and his very presence becomes your shield.

How wonderful is God's timing! For in that place of deliverance, while your enemies are still looking on, God will anoint you. It could be an anointing of healing, or an anointing of calling and direction. But, more than anything, it will be the anointing of endorsement. This anointing will be what convinces you of one thing beyond all doubt: "No matter what they say, I am Yours."

DAY 124

"Now that you know these things, you will be blessed if you do them."
JOHN 13:17

THIS verse doesn't say, "you will be blessed if you know these things." It says, "you will be blessed if you do them." In other words, it isn't enough to simply know a truth in your head. You have to live it out in your behavior. Only then will the blessing come.

Many Christians play tricks on themselves when it comes to obedience. They think they can master God's truth simply by taking a Bible class or memorizing a Scripture. Although these are good things to do, they are only the first step toward true understanding. You must believe and obey the truth in order for it to become real. It is no wonder that so many Christians become disillusioned by the lack of power in their lives. "I studied every passage on that subject, but it didn't do any good. I haven't changed a bit." Has God's truth failed? No. But you have never really walked that truth out in the real world.

The Bible says that every word of God is tested, and this includes God's Word in you. Every time you learn some aspect of God's truth in your head, God immediately sets about to test what you have learned—which simply means that He gives you an opportunity to apply your knowledge through obedience in some trying circumstance. But this is where the process too often breaks down, because obedience always costs us something. Oftentimes, we simply don't want to pay the price. Then no blessing comes, and what we have learned is lost.

It's a good idea to hear the Word; but if that's all you are doing, you are deceiving yourself. Do whatever the Word says. Make it real and tangible, so that you and all those around you can see its truth.

DAY 125

Your love has given me great joy and encouragement, because you, brother, have refreshed the hearts of the saints.
PHILEMON 1:7

WHO in your life is the most difficult to deal with on a daily basis? It could be a coworker, a callous friend, a family member, or the neighbor next door. Whoever it is, make up your mind to become a source of blessing for that person, and you'll soon find that the difficulty is no longer there. That's because you've stopped focusing on your own comfort and have begun focusing on love. One of the most joyful commands of the Christian life is the command to bless the people around us. For it is in blessing others that we ourselves receive a blessing.

Are you known as someone who brings a sense of "refreshment" to the people around you? How wonderful it would be to have people say of you that they feel refreshed just by spending time with you!

"Frankly, I just don't have the energy to think of 'creative ways' to bless others all the time," some might say. "It's too exhausting!" But the idea here is not that you give blessings all the time, out of your own strength. Instead, the point is that you are intended to become a blessing. That requires no creative forethought—but it does require a willingness to be transformed into an instrument through which God can play any time He wants.

"The memory of the righteous will be a blessing" (Proverbs 10:7).

*Blessed are those
who dwell in your house;
they are ever praising you.*
PSALM 84:4

THE most important quality of any true worshipper is that he has learned to be at ease in God's presence. The reason worship is dead in most churches today is not because the congregation does not believe in God. Instead, they just aren't comfortable being around Him. This discipline of comfort (and it is a discipline) does not come to us naturally. In fact, the opposite is true. The knee-jerk response of our sinful nature will always be to run and hide from God—just like Adam and Eve in the Garden. Therefore, the courage to seek comfort in God's presence must be built in us supernaturally through the Holy Spirit.

You can always spot people who are uncomfortable in worship; they never fail to get fidgety when God is around. Everything distracts them from focusing on the worship, which they typically find boring in any case. But the one who loves God's presence doesn't even notice the baby crying or the dog barking outside or the person with the bad cold who keeps coughing. The true worshipper has trained his focus upward.

Have you learned the discipline of being comfortable in God's presence? If not, then begin the habit of sitting before God in silence. When at last your soul can rest unguarded as you gaze on Him, you'll find that worship will spring forth on its own accord.

DAY 127

Because your love is better than life,
my lips will glorify you.
I will praise you as long as I live,
and in your name I will lift up my hands.
My soul will be satisfied as with the richest of foods;
with singing lips my mouth will praise you.
PSALM 63:3–5

WE will never be steadfast in our passion for God as long as we hold onto the notion that the goal of God's love is to give us a better life—that is, to improve our circumstances. As long as we believe this, we will continue to measure God's power by how pleasant and easy our lives are at any given moment. When conditions are good, God is good, and we are happy. But when conditions go sour, we think that God has abandoned us, and our passion for the things of God quickly dissolves.

Certainly, God wants to bless us. He is committed to healing our hurts, providing for our needs, and guiding our steps. But He doesn't do these things so that our circumstances will improve. He does it so that we will no longer live under the rule of circumstances at all.

"Your love is better than life. . . ." The psalmist is revealing the secret of spiritual stamina. In effect, he's saying, "My life is a disaster right now. I have enemies attacking me on every side. Nothing seems to be going right. But it doesn't matter, because I've learned to step out of my circumstances and abide in Your love." Once you learn to live in God's love, circumstances no longer command your attention the way they once did. Certainly, they matter, and you must deal with them. But they no longer rule you, because you no longer draw your life from them.

"My soul will be satisfied as with the richest of foods. . . ." The one who has discovered the secret of abiding in God's love experiences a continual feast for the soul. God's love is inexhaustible, and it is always spread like a banquet with a sign that reads, "This is for you."

*Meanwhile, the people
in Judah said, "The strength of the laborers
is giving out, and there is so much rubble
that we cannot rebuild the wall."
Also our enemies said,
"Before they know it or see us,
we will be right there among them and
will kill them and put an end to the work."*

NEHEMIAH 4:10–11

RESTORING Jerusalem was a dangerous and risky endeavor, and the same is true anytime we ask God to restore a broken place in our souls. The dangers always come along the same three lines— both in the case of Jerusalem and in our own circumstances.

1. "The strength of the laborers is giving out. . ." Restoration and healing take time and vigilance. They require us to make consistently good choices in an area of life where we have a habit of making bad ones. As a result, we may quickly tire of the effort. Our only defense against this exhaustion is absolute dependence on God combined with absolute belief that He is committed to our deliverance.

2. "There is so much rubble. . ." Restoration is a messy process. Before God can build His truth into our lives, He must first tear out the lies we have

believed. And this generally leaves our lives looking like a train wreck, with so much rubble strewn about that we are tempted to throw up our arms in frustration. Our only defense against such frustration is to keep our eyes focused on the one thing that God has placed before us right now. Deal with the one thing that God's Spirit is pointing at, and don't worry about the others. They will be dealt with in good time. Clearing rubble is a slow process. Be patient.

3. "Also our enemies said. . ." Satan hates the restorative work of God in our lives, and he will do anything in his power to undermine God's purpose. Nehemiah had the laborers hold a sword in one hand and a shovel in the other. And if we want to experience God's restoration, we must do the same. We are "colaborers" with Christ in the truest sense. For although we may be holding the sword and shovel, God is the one who provides the strength to dig in and fight.

DAY 129

For while we are in this tent,
we groan and are burdened,
because we do not wish to be unclothed but
to be clothed with our heavenly dwelling,
so that what is mortal may be swallowed up by life.
Now it is God who has made us for this very
purpose and has given us the Spirit as a deposit,
guaranteeing what is to come. Therefore we are
always confident and know that as long as we are
at home in the body we are away from the Lord.
We live by faith, not by sight. We are confident,
I say, and would prefer to be away from the body
and at home with the Lord. So we make it
our goal to please him, whether we are at
home in the body or away from it.
2 CORINTHIANS 5:4–9

THERE is a voice within us that continually whispers to our hearts that life is not what it was meant to be. Perhaps it is a shadow of a memory of our life before the Fall or a longing for heaven. But when we look around at life, something in us tells us, "This is not how it is supposed to be. There should be something more here—something better."

And we are right. The Bible makes clear that we do carry within our deepest hearts some awareness of the way life was supposed to be. The Bible also makes clear that this longing—this "groaning" of our souls—will never go away as long as we live in this world. Life will never fully measure up to our dreams. In a way, we are all doomed to be perpetually "homesick" for Eden. Or for heaven.

God has chosen to leave this "awareness of Eden" within our hearts—and for good reason: So that we would not get too comfortable in this fallen world; so that we would yearn for something far more grand and perfect than the best we see here; so that we would find life in what our faith can see—namely, Christ Himself—and not in the fallen trappings revealed by our physical vision.

The world is beautiful. Life is beautiful. But it is also broken. It will never measure up to the longing of our soul. As long as we keep trying to make it measure up, we will never be happy or content. The goal is not to change the world but to change the focus of our hearts. "So we make it our goal to please him, whether we are at home in the body or away from it."

For anyone who enters God's rest also rests from his own work, just as God did from his.
HEBREWS 4:10

ENTERING God's rest does allow you to rest from your own work, but that doesn't mean that you spend the rest of your life sitting around doing nothing. Instead, you enter the flow of God's work that He has already set in motion. Entering His rest is like pushing a canoe into the center of a river. You come to "rest" in the flow of power that is greater than you. If someone were to see you but not the river, you would appear to be moving with great speed and effort, while in truth you wouldn't be exerting yourself at all. You would be perfectly at rest.

Every work inspired by the Holy Spirit bears this trait of effortless power, so long as we remain in God's rest and do not try to accomplish the thing on our own. But as soon as we stop resting, and begin our "own work," what was an easy thing suddenly seems impossibly burdensome. When this happens, immediately get reconnected with God's rest.

"Now we who have believed enter that rest. . ." (Hebrews 4:3). We enter God's rest through faith, and faith is also what keeps us there. Remaining in God's rest is a matter of "trusting the river" of God's work. Do you believe that God has moved you into a particular task? Then you must continually rely on His power to accomplish it through you. If the power seems to dissipate, that doesn't mean you need to get out the oars. Rather, you need to take a break and enjoy the view.

DAY 131

When the man saw that he could not overpower him, he touched the socket of Jacob's hip so that his hip was wrenched as he wrestled with the man.
GENESIS 32:25

NOT everyone is willing to wrestle with God. In fact, the very notion of "wrestling" with our Creator seems nonsensical. "What's the point of doing such a thing?" they ask. "Besides, God will never let me down, anyway." And so the first time God does something that offends their intellect, they walk away from Him in a huff of self-righteousness. They are not willing to deal with a God who doesn't operate by their definitions of right and wrong.

We can never really know God's heart until we're willing to wrestle with Him—especially when God does something that offends us deeply, or when He doesn't do something that we thought He should have. When we wrestle with Him, of course, the goal is not to change God's ways—but rather to allow God to change us.

Anyone who wrestles with God for long will find that God has left His mark when the wrestling match is over. And God never marks you with strength, but with weakness. Notice that Jacob's encounter with God left him with a lifelong limp—but that limp was God's mark of ownership on Jacob. It was the mark that said, "I know this man. He and I have had dealings with one another. And I have chosen to fulfill My purpose through Him."

DAY 132

So Jacob called
the place Peniel, saying,
"It is because I saw God face to face,
and yet my life was spared."
GENESIS 32: 30

DO you want to have a closer relationship with God? Do you want to see His face? Very well, but don't be surprised if the "great revelation" of God's glory in your life turns out to be a wrestling match.

There is a price for intimacy with God, and the simple truth is that not many Christians are willing to pay it. Oh, we talk good about devotion to God. We may even regularly do nice things for others. But the moment the Holy Spirit begins to press uncomfortably against some sensitive area of our souls, we say, "Whoa! Hold it now. This is not what I signed up for."

Jacob could have seen God's face years before, but he was not willing to wrestle with God. For years, he tried to make deals with God instead. Sometimes God has to push us to a place of surrender so that we will wrestle with Him. And that's just what God did with Jacob. Jacob ended up at the river Jabbok (which means "to empty out"), where Jacob "emptied himself out" before God, finally surrendering his desire to strike a deal with the Almighty.

Are you asking God to reveal His face to you? Then look for the areas where it seems like God is resisting you. That is most likely where you will find Him waiting, and ready to fight. But when the fight was over, Jacob was a given a new name—and you, too, will emerge from your struggle with God with a new and shining identity, one that reflects the image of God.

DAY 133

Like a bad tooth
or a lame foot is reliance
on the unfaithful in times of trouble.
PROVERBS 25:19

BEWARE of friendships (or dating relationships) in which your friend is constantly doubting your sincerity, your honesty, or your motives. You can recognize these "doubtful" friends by these telltale signs:

- No matter what you do, they tend to assume the worst about your motives.
- They are willing to listen to (or even spread) gossip about you.
- They are quick to believe you have lied but slow to trust that you are telling the truth.

All relationships begin with some doubt and trepidation. Even the Proverbs tell us the "righteous man is cautious in friendship" (12:26). But we are not wise to tolerate friendships or dating relationships with people who never seem to move past their doubts about us. Such people constantly need to be convinced of our sincerity; they repeatedly demand that we prove our love. And the Word tells us that, when any real trouble hits our lives, these unfaithful friends will become a hindrance to our victory, bringing us nothing but pain.

It is right and good to believe in people and to fight for relationships. But there is great wisdom in recognizing unfaithful friends and making the difficult choice to prune them out of our lives.

DAY 134

"Their deeds do not permit them to return to their God."

HOSEA 5:4

"AND do not grieve the Holy Spirit of God. . ." (Ephesians 4:30). We often forget that the Holy Spirit is a person; and when our actions grieve Him, He withdraws the manifestation of His presence from our lives. On this point, we often fool ourselves into thinking that some sins create more separation than others. "I don't deny that this thing I do is wrong. But I don't think it really interferes that much with my relationship with God. It's just a little thing, after all. I don't think it really matters."

But it does matter, more than you realize.

Beware of clinging to "pet sins" as though they were harmless. They aren't. They unravel our intimate communion with God, one thread at a time. And they prevent us from enjoying free intimacy with God, even when that's what we sincerely desire. "Their deeds do not permit them to return to their

God." Examine your deeds. Are there "pet sins" that you've allowed to take root in your behavior on a regular basis? If so, you can be sure they have created a wall of division between you and the Holy Spirit. Ask God's forgiveness for the "little sins," and then drop them from your life. Once you do, God will begin to build a closeness between you that is deeper than you previously imagined possible.

"You have been faithful with a few things; I will put you in charge of many things" (Matthew 25:21).

DAY 135

Endure hardship as discipline;
God is treating you as sons.
For what son is not disciplined by his father?
If you are not disciplined (and everyone undergoes
discipline), then you are illegitimate children and not
true sons. Moreover, we have all had human fathers
who disciplined us and we respected them for it.
How much more should we submit to
the Father of our spirits and live!
HEBREWS 12:7–9

WE all want to be taught by God, until He actually starts doing it. And suddenly we think God doesn't have the slightest idea of how to go about teaching us at all! "If God would just do this one thing for me," you say, "then I would have no trouble trusting Him with everything else." Yes you would.

How arrogant we are to think that we know what we need better than God does! If God is not answering your prayer in the way you wish, it is precisely because you do not need that prayer answered in that way—regardless of how fervently you believe you do. Never trust your own appraisal of what you need from God. Instead, trust Him. He knows your heart perfectly; He knows your needs perfectly. And the methods He employs in teaching you His ways are perfectly suited for both.

"But I don't understand the point He's trying to make by allowing this trial," you say. "What good is His teaching if I never understand what He wants me to learn?" You will understand, if you do not lose heart.

We must be patient and trust Him. In time, we will understand—and that understanding will be worth whatever pain or confusion we had to endure in the process. This is God's promise to us. "No discipline seems pleasant at the time, but painful. Later on, however, it produces a harvest of righteousness and peace for those who have been trained by it" (Hebrews 12:11).

DAY 136

So do not throw away your confidence;
it will be richly rewarded.
You need to persevere so that when you have done
the will of God, you will receive what he has promised.
For in just a very little while, "He who is coming
will come and will not delay. But my righteous
one will live by faith. And if he shrinks back,
I will not be pleased with him." But we are
not of those who shrink back and are destroyed,
but of those who believe and are saved.
HEBREWS 10:35–39

ONE of the biggest problems with postmodern Christians is that they give up on God far too easily. They have faith, but only for a week or two. If no results appear in that time, then these hurry-up Christians shrug their shoulders, and then off they go to try to build a life on something else.

More than any generation before us, we have learned to value instant results. In fact, we demand it—even in our gods. As a generation, we continually search for gods that are "fast-acting" and bring us immediate satisfaction. But to our disappointment, we find that God's grace is slow by our standards; sometimes it's as slow moving as a glacier. And so we quickly become disillusioned with pursuing Him, and we go looking for better alternatives.

Only there are none. There is only one way to see God's promises fulfilled in our lives, and that is by clinging to the tenacious confidence that God will come through, no matter how things look right now: God will deliver me; God will show me the way; God will reveal Himself to me. And it doesn't matter what happens around me, or what anyone says to convince me otherwise. I have set my heart, and nothing will sway me.

This is not the way of our generation. But it the only way to receive the promise of God. And remember—those slow-moving glaciers carved entire mountain ranges across our earth.

DAY 137

"You believe at last!" Jesus answered.
"But a time is coming, and has come,
when you will be scattered, each to his own home.
You will leave me all alone. Yet I am not alone,
for my Father is with me. I have told you
these things, so that in me you may have peace.
In this world you will have trouble.
But take heart! I have overcome the world."
JOHN 16:31–33

OFTENTIMES we are surprised and ashamed by our own capacity to abandon God in times of personal stress. Just when we think we've grown up a bit, something happens to shake up our world, and we immediately flee from God's presence in order to fix the problem on our own. After all this time, we still think we can handle some things better with our own strength.

But, of course, we can't. And, like Jesus' disciples, despite our most valiant attempts to overcome on our own, we inevitably soon find ourselves huddled in some dark corner, hiding in fear from an enemy that is too powerful for us.

Jesus says, "Although you believe now, I know the time will come when you will doubt Me. You will abandon Me and try to fight the world on your own. And you will lose. When that happens, come hide in Me. I will keep you safe. And you will learn again how to win through Me."

Jesus never promised that we would overcome the world. In fact, He said we couldn't. "In this world you will have trouble," He warned—but He promised that He has overcome the world for us, so that as we abide in Him we, too, will overcome.

The next time trouble comes, stop yourself before you do anything. Ask, "Am I about to run to God, or away from Him?" Then make up your mind to remain at peace in Christ, trusting Him to overcome on your behalf.

*So Naaman went with his horses
and chariots and stopped at the door
of Elisha's house. Elisha sent a messenger to say to
him, "Go, wash yourself seven times in the Jordan,
and your flesh will be restored and you will be
cleansed." But Naaman went away angry and said,
"I thought that he would surely come out to me
and stand and call on the name of the LORD his God,
wave his hand over the spot and cure me of my
leprosy. Are not Abana and Pharpar, the rivers of
Damascus, better than any of the waters of Israel?
Couldn't I wash in them and be cleansed?"
So he turned and went off in a rage.*

2 KINGS 5:9–12

GOD was interested in curing far more than Naaman's leprosy. He was also interested in curing Naaman's pride. In fact, God dealt with the pride first. That's generally the way God's healing goes— first the soul, then the body. He wouldn't heal Naaman's physical illness until the man first dealt with the illness in his heart. And what do you suppose would have happened if Naaman had never humbled himself? He would have kept his leprosy and blamed it all on God's lack of power or His lack of compassion.

When we ask God for healing, often we're asking

God to heal the wrong thing first. There is an order to God's healing work in our lives, and it almost always goes from the inside out. God may lay our physical healing aside in order to deal with a deeper sickness lodged within our hearts.

Naaman's real illness was pride. And that illness very nearly kept him from receiving the physical healing Elisha offered. Are you struggling with illness or pain in your body? Don't rush to ask for God to heal you. Instead, ask Him to search your heart for illnesses you didn't know were there.

DAY 139

In the same way,
the Spirit helps us in our weakness.
We do not know what we ought to pray for,
but the Spirit himself intercedes for us
with groans that words cannot express.
And he who searches our hearts knows the
mind of the Spirit, because the Spirit intercedes
for the saints in accordance with God's will.
ROMANS 8:26–27

HAVE you ever felt an ache in your soul that you could not name? You long, you hurt, you yearn for something deep within your heart, but you don't know what it is. You do not know what you need; you know only that you need. You want to cry to God in prayer, but when you come before Him, you find that you have nothing to say. Or, rather, there is nothing in your heart that words can say. That is when we must rely on the Holy Spirit to intercede. For though we cannot name our pain, He can. He alone knows what we need. And He knows how to translate our hearts before the throne of God.

We must not think of prayer as a matter of words but rather a connection between our heart and God's. Once we begin to think of prayer in this way, then we discover that everything we do can be transformed into prayer—as long as we keep our hearts focused on God.

There will always be times when words fail us, but that never means we should stop praying. In fact, those are the very times when we need to pray the most. For it is in those times, when "words cannot express" your heart, that your heart most desperately needs to be heard. Pour out your heart in silence, or in sighing, or in "groans that words cannot express," but never fail to pour it out all the same. Maintain the connection between your heart and God's. He will never fail to hear and understand.

DAY 140

We demolish arguments
and every pretension that sets itself up against
the knowledge of God, and we take captive
every thought to make it obedient to Christ.
2 CORINTHIANS 10:5

SPIRITUAL warfare is a given. It happens to every Christian. Every day. But, amazingly, lots of Christians pretend it doesn't happen at all. They adopt the childish notion that says, "If I close my eyes, then you can't see me." In other words, they believe that if they pay no attention to the spiritual battle raging around them, then it won't really have any impact on their lives.

Paul never questions whether or not spiritual warfare is real. He assumes that it is, and that we are of necessity engaged in it. His only thought is how we should fight, and what our objectives should be.

Ignoring spiritual warfare is as dangerous as a soldier walking along the front lines of battle pretending there is no war. That soldier will be one of the first casualties, and the same is true for Christians who pretend that Satan and his forces aren't really out to destroy them after all.

"But I don't know how to fight!" you may say. Then you must make up your mind to learn. The strongholds of Satan are always built on lies, often lies that are very close to the truth. So that is where you must begin. What lies do you believe—about yourself, about others, about the world around you, about God and the church? "How can I know that?" you ask. Well, the only way to gain the skill to spot a counterfeit dollar bill is by studying the authentic bill until you know it by heart. The same principle applies to spotting counterfeit beliefs. And so you learn to recognize Satan's lies by studying what is true—that is, God's Word.

DAY 141

When the people saw that Moses was so long in coming down from the mountain, they gathered around Aaron and said, "Come, make us gods who will go before us. As for this fellow Moses who brought us up out of Egypt, we don't know what has happened to him."

EXODUS 32:1

WHEN you pray for guidance, and God doesn't answer right away, how do you react? Are you willing to wait until God comes, even if it's a very long time?

When it comes to waiting on God, most of us

are like the people of Israel. We'll give God some time, maybe even an unreasonable amount of time. But if He doesn't show up, we eventually decide we can't wait any longer. And we set off to find another god to follow—for a while anyway. We don't want to wait anymore.

But God knows that waiting tests our resolve. Do you really believe God's deliverance is your only hope? Do you really believe God loves you? If you believe these two things, then you will wait however long it takes, and you won't be looking around for alternative lesser gods to go after.

Waiting purifies us; it brings the dross of our souls to the surface more quickly than anything else in the spiritual life. For instance, the dross of doubt and pride says, "I'll put my confidence in God up to a point. But if He doesn't show up by next Tuesday, then I'll take matters into my own hands." God will "show up" when He needs to, not when you think He must. How many times have we begged God to act before we reach some horrible deadline, and only when He finally does appear do we see that our deadline really didn't matter in the least? He takes a bigger view of things than we possibly can. And He is present even when we cannot see Him.

> But Moses sought
> the favor of the LORD his God.
> "O LORD," he said, "why should your anger burn
> against your people, whom you brought out
> of Egypt with great power and a mighty hand?
> Why should the Egyptians say, 'It was with evil
> intent that he brought them out, to kill them
> in the mountains and to wipe them off the face
> of the earth'? Turn from your fierce anger;
> relent and do not bring disaster on your people.
> Remember your servants Abraham, Isaac and
> Israel, to whom you swore by your own self:
> 'I will make your descendants as numerous as
> the stars in the sky and I will give your descendants
> all this land I promised them, and it will be
> their inheritance forever.'" Then the LORD relented
> and did not bring on his people the disaster
> he had threatened.

EXODUS 32:11–14

WE have no concept of our own capacity to impact the heart of God. Here, in these verses, one man sways God from destroying an entire nation. How much more can we influence God toward showing mercy to the lost people around us? Or to our cities and families? Or to our society as a whole?

Never underestimate the depth to which your

prayers can impact God's heart to act. Of course, we should never think that our job in prayer is to goad God to be compassionate to the broken, or to hold Him back from wreaking havoc on the world of sinners. The very idea is ridiculous! How could we as God's creation know more about compassion than the God who created us?

God is loving and merciful on His own accord, far more than we are. But He has formed a wild and seemingly reckless partnership with His body, the Church. He has selected us as the "enforcers" of His mercy, His compassion, and His love. In effect, that means that sometimes God holds back His compassion until we are moved with compassion. There are times He will not act until we pray. "I tell you the truth, whatever you bind on earth will be bound in heaven, and whatever you loose on earth will be loosed in heaven" (Matthew 18:18).

Never grow slack in intercession for others. You never know what great act of mercy God is waiting to perform.

In all the travels of the Israelites, whenever the cloud lifted from above the tabernacle, they would set out; but if the cloud did not lift, they did not set out—until the day it lifted. So the cloud of the LORD was over the tabernacle by day, and fire was in the cloud by night, in the sight of all the house of Israel during all their travels.

EXODUS 40:36–38

YOU can always tell when the presence of God has moved on from a job or calling to which He originally led you. Everything that was once easy is suddenly burdensome and hard. Things that used to energize you now drain you to the dregs. And, mostly, you no longer sense God's glory in anything you do. "But didn't God call me to do this?" you wonder. Yes, of course. But now He is calling you somewhere else. Once God's presence has moved on, you would do well not to hang around either, any longer than necessary, however settled you have become. Pack up your things, find out where God's Spirit is going, and follow Him there.

Sometimes you'll find Christians clinging to jobs or callings from which God's glory lifted years ago. Beware of loving your calling or your comfort more than you love God. If you do, you won't even notice when God's glory leaves. And you'll be lost in a dead work.

Other Christians, of course, have the opposite

problem. They get the itch to go before God does. We must discipline our hearts to keep pace with God—going neither behind nor ahead of His timing in matters of jobs or callings or anything else. To do this, we need to focus on God's Spirit and not on our personal preferences. Learn to be at peace wherever God has you. "I know what it is to be in need, and I know what it is to have plenty. I have learned the secret of being content in any and every situation, whether well fed or hungry, whether living in plenty or in want. I can do everything through him who gives me strength" (Philippians 4:12–13).

DAY 144

Though the fig tree does not bud
and there are no grapes on the vines,
though the olive crop fails and the fields
produce no food, though there are no sheep in the pen
and no cattle in the stalls, yet I will rejoice in the
LORD, I will be joyful in God my Savior. The
Sovereign LORD is my strength; he makes my feet like
the feet of a deer, he enables me to go on the heights.
HABAKKUK 3:17–19

HOW different these verses are from the response most of us have when life doesn't go the way we want. . .

"How could God abandon me like this?"

"Why would God let this happen to me?"

"What do I have to do to get God to change this?"

"I'd rather die than live in these conditions."

But reacting this way to life's troubles doesn't get us anywhere with God. In fact, the only thing these attitudes accomplish is to reveal that on some level at least we are still clinging to the notion that fulfillment springs from our circumstances. But this, of course, is not true at all. We can gain enjoyment from our circumstances but never lasting joy. We may find tranquil moments in our circumstances but never lasting peace. A circumstance may make us feel alive, but it can never give us abundant life.

These eternal things—joy, peace, abundant life—spring from eternal sources. They are never dependant on circumstance. This is why the prophet could say, "It doesn't matter what happens in my circumstances. Even if everything falls apart, yet I will rejoice in God, because my life comes from Him. And what a wondrous life it is!" "He makes my feet like the feet of a deer, He enables me to go on the heights."

The fact is that life in this world may never live up to our dreams. There will always be disappointments and even tragedies that we must face. But for those who draw their life from God, no circumstance, however fierce, can steal their joy away.

Find your life in God, and your circumstances will immediately lose the power to ruin you.

DAY 145

My heart is not proud,
O LORD, my eyes are not haughty;
I do not concern myself with great
matters or things too wonderful for me.
But I have stilled and quieted my soul;
like a weaned child with its mother,
like a weaned child is my soul within me.
O Israel, put your hope in the LORD
both now and forevermore.

PSALM 131:1–3

THERE is a simplicity that comes to those who walk with God for any length of time. A quietness of soul, a stillness of thoughts marks them. You can see the calm on their faces. Their faces are free from concern. Through the discipline of the Lord, they have learned peace (Hebrews 12:11). Through the struggle toward obedience, they have learned humility. Through the things they have suffered, they have learned how to still and quiet their souls and rest upon the breast of God. They have learned to be children again.

There is a reason why you keep fighting your sinful nature, fighting the world, fighting to believe in an unseen God. Through your efforts, God is storing treasure in your soul: Simple life. Abundant life. Life that does not concern itself with matters too big for it to understand. Life that trusts God implicitly and, in that trust, finds unshakeable peace.

You are seeking the life of Christ, flowing freely through you. In all your struggles, in all your effort, do not forget that goal. Do not forget Him.

Lay down your pride. Stop troubling yourself with things that are too big for you. Just let them go. Calm and quiet your soul before God. And look to Jesus. "Those who look to him are radiant; their faces are never covered with shame" (Psalm 34:5).

DAY 146

*Praise be to the God and Father
of our Lord Jesus Christ,
who has blessed us in the heavenly realms
with every spiritual blessing in Christ.*

EPHESIANS 1:3

YOU may ask, "What is a spiritual blessing anyway?" These are blessings related to things in the spiritual realm—such as love, peace, joy, and all the other fruit of the Spirit, as well as spiritual gifts and spiritual power. In essence, spiritual blessings are the attributes that give meaning to our physical lives. Very often we come to God begging Him to bless us with peace or joy or some other fruit of the Spirit, and we don't understand that God already answered that prayer long ago. He has laid His blessing out for us as a gift. That's all He can do, short of forcing it on us (which He won't do, even if we beg Him to). It's up to us to receive His blessings into our hearts through faith. When we ask God to bless us with spiritual blessings, our request makes no sense spiritually, since we're asking Him to give us something He's already given us.

Notice that God has given us not just a few blessings, or a fair number of blessings; He has given us every one of them. God has already blessed us with every spiritual blessing there is—so that we are in a state of perpetual blessedness. We are blessed.

"Why, then, don't I feel blessed?" you ask. Sometimes it is because we don't understand that the blessings of God are already ours. And sometimes it is because we fixate on blessings that God never promised to give—usually, some sort of physical blessing. Many times, we complain that God has not blessed us, when in reality we mean that He has not given us money, success, fame, marriage, children, beauty, or physical perfection. Ultimately, such things cannot bring us life. They are not true blessings. And when we fixate on them, we inevitably miss all the spiritual blessings God has already provided.

*For this reason,
ever since I heard about your faith in the
Lord Jesus and your love for all the saints,
I have not stopped giving thanks for you,
remembering you in my prayers. I keep asking
that the God of our Lord Jesus Christ,
the glorious Father, may give you the Spirit
of wisdom and revelation, so that you may know
him better. I pray also that the eyes of your heart
may be enlightened in order that you may know the
hope to which he has called you, the riches of
his glorious inheritance in the saints, and his
incomparably great power for us who believe. . . .*

EPHESIANS 1:15–19

LOVE is tenacious by its very nature. It follows then that our commitment to love our Christian brothers and sisters must, of necessity, be resolved to the point of stubbornness. We are called to hope unendingly on their behalf, and to believe unreservedly in the best that God has for them—until God's abundant life spreads into every part of their souls.

This tenacity of faith and love is woven into Paul's prayer: "I have not stopped. . .I keep asking. . ." It takes a stubborn faith to pray this way. People will always let you down. They will often do things or say things that injure you deeply. But when we are hurt, we are not to stop believing on behalf of our Christian brothers and sisters. For our faith is not in the people, but in the power of God's Spirit at work in their lives.

Many of us have given up on some of the Christians we know. The fact that we've given up on them is not a bad reflection on them, however, but on us. Are they not still our brothers and our sisters? Are they not destined to be conformed to the likeness of Christ? Then why are we no longer believing God on their behalf? Why have you judged our brothers and sisters?

"If I. . .have not love, I am nothing." (1 Corinthians 13:2). Beware of letting your personal injuries and human opinions overrule God's command to love. You may be right. But if you do not love, then all your "rightness" amounts to nothing.

DAY 148

For we are God's workmanship,
created in Christ Jesus to do good works,
which God prepared in advance for us to do.
EPHESIANS 2:10

FEW of us realize the extraordinary and unique beauty that lies within each of us. We tend to think of ourselves as "pretty much like everyone else," but this is a very shortsighted view of reality. It would be like saying that one symphony is pretty much the same as any other. Anyone who believes that has obviously not listened to many symphonies.

An extraordinary beauty lies within you that is uniquely your own. It may be quiet or grand, gentle or strong, simple or multifaceted—or a mixture of a thousand different qualities. But it is your beauty. It has never come before in anyone else, and it will never come again. It is yours.

This unique beauty is the image of God that He created in each of our hearts. We are each like a different symphony, a living sculpture like no other, created by the hand of the master artist. I cannot play your song, and you cannot play mine. We are gifts from God to one another—songs He sings to us through each other.

Once you accept that you are God's workmanship—that is, God's artwork—then the first thing that happens is you finally begin to relax; you stop trying to be something you're not. Once you do, you begin to see what an amazing artist God really is.

DAY 149

I pray that out of his glorious riches
he may strengthen you with power
through his Spirit in your inner being,
so that Christ may dwell in your hearts through faith.
And I pray that you, being rooted and established
in love, may have power, together with all the saints,
to grasp how wide and long and high and deep is the
love of Christ, and to know this love that surpasses
knowledge——that you may be filled to the
measure of all the fullness of God.
EPHESIANS 3:16–19

NO one can receive a revelation of God's love and not be changed, not when that revelation is personal, intended just for you. You can study God's love as a concept for decades and even come to believe in it in an abstract sense, but it will do no good for your soul. It is the personal revelation of His love that transforms us. When the simple, profound message— "God loves me"—first comes alive in your innermost being, the power of that love comes and breathes new life into your soul. Your eyes are opened, your heart is enlarged, and you are able to take in the world from God's compassionate point of view. Your heart comes alive, and you suddenly find within you a reservoir of love that was never there before. The revelation of God's love has come in and created that deep well of love. (See 1 John 4:19.) Now you can pass God's love on to others.

God's love, or rather the revelation of His love, is God's agent for transformation in our lives. Before we can take hold of the fullness of Christ, we must first take hold of the fact that He loves us. It is through God's love that we come to know Him. The revelation of God's love is what brought us to Christ in the first place, and that same ongoing revelation makes room for God to live and manifest Himself in our lives. Until you trust that God loves you in the most personal and intimate sense possible, your soul will never find its way to God's power and presence.

His love makes all things new—and that includes us. If we could only grasp God's love for us in its fullness, we would be the happiest and most powerful people in the world.

DAY 150

As a prisoner for the Lord,
then, I urge you to live a life
worthy of the calling you have received.
Be completely humble and gentle; be patient,
bearing with one another in love. Make every effort to
keep the unity of the Spirit through the bond of peace.
EPHESIANS 4:1–3

TO be a follower of Christ is a high calling, far higher than we typically realize or allow ourselves to think. A follower of Christ is a marked person, one whose manner in life is so obviously and consistently different that it stands out in conspicuous contrast to the fallen world around it.

Ask yourself: Is my life marked by the Spirit of God? That is, what do people notice most about me as they get to know me? And when I leave a particular job or city, what is the thing those folks will most remember about me? That I am a funny or serious, a hard worker or friendly? Or that I was different in some way?

We each have many fine qualities, but they are not what "mark" us as belonging to God. What people notice most about "marked" Christians is not their personality at all, but their humility and their love. These are people who are consistently gentle, patient, and forbearing with others. They are committed to unity and not division—which is to say they do not demand their own way, nor do they insist that everyone around them agree with their opinions. They do not slander.

We never become a "marked" people through our own efforts. Rather, as we submit ourselves to God, His Spirit marks us. Only one man ever truly lived the Christian life in the proper way, and that was Christ Himself. That is why living a "marked" life generally boils down to getting yourself out of the way so Jesus is free to live through you by His Spirit. "He must become greater; I must become less" (John 3:30).

DAY 151

It was he who gave some to be apostles, some to be prophets, some to be evangelists, and some to be pastors and teachers, to prepare God's people for works of service, so that the body of Christ may be built up until we all reach unity in the faith and in the knowledge of the Son of God and become mature, attaining to the whole measure of the fullness of Christ.
EPHESIANS 4:11–13

GOD has given you spiritual gifts for one purpose alone, and that is to prepare God's people for works of service. You were not given spiritual gifts so you could make a name for yourself or build a reputation as a "gifted" person. And you certainly were not given spiritual gifts so you could wield control over people or make money off them.

The fact is this: The gifts God has given you are not really for you at all. Instead, they are for His church. You are simply the courier—a carrier of God's gifts, not their owner. God has chosen you as the instrument of delivery, but the gifts are for His body.

Because of this, you must be careful not to use your spiritual gift for any purpose other than those prescribed by Scripture. Always keep an eye on your motives. Am I employing my spiritual gift to serve others—or to serve myself in some way? Am I using my gift to build someone up—or to "put them in their place"? Am I using the gifts God has given me in a way that brings glory to me instead of to God?

You can know whether you are using God's gifts rightly by observing the fruit they produce. Are people encouraged by your gifts? Are they provoked to seek God and to study His Word? Are they being equipped to serve others? Or do they walk away from you feeling condemned, misunderstood, like a failure?

God never intended His gifts to be used to beat up His children but to bless them. Are your gifts a blessing to others? If not, then stop whatever you're doing immediately, and ask the Holy Spirit to show you His "more excellent way" (1 Corinthians 12:31).

Then we will no longer be infants,
tossed back and forth by the waves,
and blown here and there by every wind
of teaching and by the cunning and craftiness
of men in their deceitful scheming. Instead, speaking
the truth in love, we will in all things grow up into
him who is the Head, that is, Christ.

EPHESIANS 4:14–15

SPEAKING the truth in love is an art. It takes discipline and practice to get it right. But ultimately, the ability to do it well comes not from skill but from motive. You might know how to confront someone in a nice way, but if your heart is not right in the matter, you will still fall short of speaking the truth in love. It's more likely that you will speak the truth "in anger," or "in jealousy," or "in manipulation." If you speak "in love," you must speak from a heart of compassion—a heart that's free from other motives such as fear, resentment, or the selfish desire to control someone else's behavior. When the truth we share springs out of the pure desire to love, only then can we say we're speaking the truth in love. Anything less than that is just an exercise in pretension.

That's why it takes so much practice to learn how to speak the truth in love—because the motives of our hearts are the key to doing it right, and we need practice to discern them. The truth is that we cannot speak the truth in love unless we've first taken the time to examine all our reasons for speaking in the first place. Are we trying to "correct" someone because his behavior might lead him into danger (spiritually or otherwise)—or because his behavior irritates us? Are we really trying to love by talking to her about her sin—or does our motivation lie in the fact that her particular sin makes our lives more difficult? We must take the time to examine ourselves and get our own hearts straight long before we start a crusade to correct the "evil" we see in those around us.

Speaking the truth in love can be a powerful weapon against confusion, both in the church and in our personal relationships. But the truth must always be rooted in God's unselfish love.

DAY 153

"In your anger do not sin":
Do not let the sun go down
while you are still angry.
EPHESIANS 4:26

ANGER is not a sin, although many Christians today seem to think it is. Anger is simply an emotion—just as sorrow or giddiness or boredom are emotions.

More than that, anger is a good emotion, useful in its place. Never allowing yourself to be angry is the same as never allowing yourself to laugh or to cry. They are all perfectly acceptable expressions of what it means to be human.

Nevertheless, some Christians suppress their anger relentlessly—because they are afraid their anger might lead them to do something they'll regret. Unfortunately, suppressing anger does nothing to make us more godly—it just makes us more religious.

The truth is that just about everything we feel might lead to temptation. "Don't feel sad! It might lead you to depression!" "Don't be too happy! It might lead you to complacency." As illogical as the idea sounds in these contexts, many find this approach perfectly reasonable when it comes to anger "Don't get angry! It might make you say or do something you'll regret."

Well, yes. . .in fact, it might. But anger can also be a godly emotion. When God gets angry, it is always as a reaction to injustice—committed either against Him or against His children. Likewise, when an injustice is committed—either against us or against someone we love—it is good and right to be angry about it. Righteous anger calls out injustice and condemns it. That sort of anger is very godlike indeed.

Anger is one of the most important defenses our souls have against injustice. Therefore, never let anyone convince you that your anger is wrong. Rather, "in your anger do not sin."

DAY 154

For you were once darkness,
but now you are light in the Lord.
Live as children of light (for the fruit of the light
consists in all goodness, righteousness and truth)
and find out what pleases the Lord.
EPHESIANS 5:8–10

THE discovery of God's heart, and thus His will, rarely comes to us the way we expect, or even in the way we wish it would. "I want to learn how to please the Lord!" we say easily enough, but we don't want to learn in the way God wants to teach. We want epiphanies—divine encounters rich with thunder and lightning and all the things we think make God believable. And in those encounters, we want to hear God explain Himself to us. "Tell me what pleases You!" we cry—and sometimes God will answer these cries on the spot. But it is usually better for us if He doesn't. Too often we think we need God to tell us something, when what we really need is to pay attention to what He is showing us through His silence.

The discovery of God's heart is not an event but an ongoing journey. It is a journey of wonder and struggle, fear and desire. The journey itself is the instrument through which God most often reveals His heart to us. But even then His revelation is not obvious. We have to search Him out.

Sometimes, in the midst of hard times, we reach out for God and cannot find Him. "Where are You, God, in the midst of this circumstance?" we plead. He is there, we know, but just beyond our grasp—and this, it seems, is the way He wants things to be.

"But why?" We almost never find the answer to this until later, after the struggle has passed. We did our best, we've made it through, and a measure of peace has now returned to our souls. Only then, when we turn around, do we suddenly see Jesus standing there, where He has been all along. And,we find we know Him in ways we never expected.

This is the gift that comes through struggles. We were learning to know Him better all along, even when we did not know it.

DAY 155

"Ah, Sovereign LORD,
you have made the heavens and the earth
by your great power and outstretched arm.
Nothing is too hard for you."
JEREMIAH 32:17

LOOK around and consider the greatness of our God! Look at the clouds—He makes each one unique, and yet every one of them conveys impressions of His majesty. Look at the mountains, how old and solid, beautiful and firm they are to us. God created each one with nothing but a word—and yet how they speak to us of His mystery and His dangerous, wild glory. Look at the ocean—its vastness is too great for us to truly comprehend, and yet it gives us some hint of eternity, for it does not age as other things do. It remains unchanged since the beginning. In its depth, we gain some hint of the depths of God. And yet for God, it is a small matter to create an ocean. For Him, it is a small matter to create a universe.

And all these things He created for our benefit—so that we could see in them something of His nature, the infinity of His power. . .and His infinitely creative love.

No one can spend time considering the grandness of God and still keep worrying about lesser things. The revelation of God's greatness is woven into His creation for our benefit and His glory. It's there for you to see, if you will just take the time to look.

The next time you are overcome with worry, lie down in the grass outside and spend half an hour looking up at the stars. Can't the God who lovingly created this also take care of you? There is hope built into those stars, if you will see it. And when you do, you will forget your worry and confess to your creator, "Ah, Sovereign Lord, You have made the heavens and the earth by Your great power and outstretched arm. Nothing is too hard for You."

*I will lead the blind
by ways they have not known,
along unfamiliar paths I will guide them;
I will turn the darkness into light before them and
make the rough places smooth. These are the things
I will do; I will not forsake them.*

ISAIAH 42:16

WE are all blind in our own way, usually in a great many ways. The sooner we accept that about ourselves, the less surprised we will be when God begins to lead us into places that seem to us dark and unfamiliar. For He certainly will take us to such places—pitch black places, where we cannot see a thing. Of course, the place God is leading us is not dark at all—it's as bright and clear as day to Him. But it is dark to us, because it is an area of blindness for us. It is unfamiliar, uncharted, and, quite often, not at all where we would choose to go. But that is only because our blindness keeps us from seeing it as it really is. God knows there are treasures there, which we cannot see, that He wants us to have. "I will give you the treasures of darkness, riches stored in secret places, so that you may know that I am the LORD, the God of Israel, who summons you by name" (Isaiah 45:3).

God takes us to the dark places not to frighten us but to open our eyes so we may see. He wants to "turn the darkness into light" before us. Once He heals us, we see that the darkness was never really dark at all, and so we no longer fear it. Soon, we begin to look around this new place for the first time, and we find treasures here we never saw before.

Do not be afraid to travel with God in the dark, where even He is invisible to your eyes. When the time is right, He will restore your vision, and you will see the reason that He brought you here. The treasures will be suddenly obvious.

DAY 157

"Come, all you who are thirsty, come to the waters;
and you who have no money, come, buy and eat!
Come, buy wine and milk without money and
without cost. Why spend money on what is not bread,
and your labor on what does not satisfy?
Listen, listen to me, and eat what is good, and your
soul will delight in the richest of fare. Give ear and
come to me; hear me, that your soul may live."
ISAIAH 55:1–3

GOD has created within us a hunger we cannot easily name. It is a tickling thirst at the back of our souls, ever building through the years the longer it goes unquenched. We know it is there, though we cannot name it, and we spend our years doing everything we can imagine to try to fill it. It is God's homing beacon, set right in the core of our hearts. And it is one of the greatest evidences on earth that God is real.

Watch any person long enough, and you will begin to see the hunger and thirst of his or her soul expressed. Perhaps he is caught up in the pursuit of worldly success—but why? Because he hopes it will bring him life. Or perhaps she is killing herself in order to be beautiful—but why? For the same reason. We all crave life—which is to say we all crave God—so much that we will try nearly anything to get it. Of course, we do not want to believe that it is God we crave. We'd much rather believe that we crave something smaller, something we can control. And Satan is there, ready to offer a whole cafeteria of counterfeit nourishment for our souls.

But it is God we crave, and nothing less will satisfy. All of the counterfeits that Satan offers have one common trait—they lose their appeal over time. But not so with God. The more of Him we taste, the more we desire.

Where are you getting the food for your soul? Your job? Your friends? Your romantic relationships? Ultimately, they will all run dry. They can never quench the hunger deep inside.

You thirst for God.

DAY 158

"The wind blows wherever it pleases.
You hear its sound, but you cannot tell
where it comes from or where it is going.
So it is with everyone born of the Spirit."
JOHN 3:8

THE workings of God's Spirit within us are always cloaked in mystery. We feel a call, an urging, somewhere deep within us. But we don't know where it comes from, or where it will lead. And until we become comfortable with that mystery, we will never obey. Until we can embrace God's mystery, we can never learn to follow the Spirit well.

His Spirit will always be a mystery—He is like a wind blowing through our souls. Who can say how that happens? Who can "deconstruct" God's way with our souls? It is a romance, a union of two spirits into one.

The Spirit is that wind that leads you right now, in this moment, directing you one step at a time. You may look to where the wind is blowing, and you will see dozens of places He could take you. But, then again, the wind may shift before you reach there, and suddenly you feel a push to go another way altogether. "But it all seems so risky," you say. "What if I go the wrong way?" Risky to whom? You—or God? God knows where He is leading you.

Your only command is to follow in faith.

The Holy Spirit calls us to embrace God's mystery. His breezes lead us to a place where we must decide we no longer need to know all the answers. All we need is to stay close to Him, following without hesitation wherever He leads. Once we make that choice, we soon discover that we wouldn't want to follow God in any less romantic way.

DAY 159

Not that I have already obtained all this, or have already been made perfect, but I press on to take hold of that for which Christ Jesus took hold of me. Brothers, I do not consider myself yet to have taken hold of it. But one thing I do: Forgetting what is behind and straining toward what is ahead, I press on toward the goal to win the prize for which God has called me heavenward in Christ Jesus.

PHILIPPIANS 3:12–14

HAVE you allowed Jesus to take hold of you in the way He took hold of Paul? God wants to reveal Himself to you, including His will for your life—but first, He requires your absolute surrender. Of course, we don't like this approach to discovering God's will at all, because it forces us to trust God in ways we'd rather not. We'd rather God would provide us a detailed description of His purpose for our lives and then give us some time to consider His proposal before we accept. But God will not work this way. All attempts to negotiate an alternative approach with God will fail.

We expect that the loss of control will make us worry a great deal. "What will God do?" "Where will He lead?" "Will I like what He chooses for me?" But when we finally do surrender everything to God, we find our hearts become peaceful, quite the opposite of what we expected to happen. Peace comes to the surrendered soul—a peace that passes understanding, because it is the peace of a child at rest in his father's arms. The child does not know why he trusts his father; he simply does so implicitly. When we allow God to "take hold" of us fully in this way, a similar sort of peace comes over us. A great many things that used to concern us suddenly become irrelevant. The only thing that matters is staying close to God, because we have placed our trust in Him.

Do you know this kind of "childlike" peace? If not, perhaps it's time you stopped trying to negotiate with God and simply surrendered to Him. "I tell you the truth, unless you change and become like little children, you will never enter the kingdom of heaven" (Matthew 18:3).

*When the perishable
has been clothed with the imperishable,
and the mortal with immortality,
then the saying that is written will come true:
"Death has been swallowed up in victory."
"Where, O death, is your victory?
Where, O death, is your sting?"*

1 CORINTHIANS 15:54–55

WHEN most people think of death, they naturally think of physical death. But there are many different kinds of death, several of which are far more terrifying to us than the death of our physical bodies. For example, there is the death of hope. People cannot live without hope, and the one whose hope is dead or dying considers physical death of no great importance. There is also the death of joy. Some who are joyless welcome physical death when it comes; since life has become such a burden. And there are many other kinds of death besides these—the death of freedom, the death of passion, and the death of any of our emotions. There are as many forms of death as there are qualities in us.

Every fear that plagues us is some expression of our fear of death. We fear the death of a relationship, the death of other's respect for us, the death of beauty in our body or in our soul. Death is our great nemesis;

the terrible legacy that sin has brought to us.

The point is this: When Jesus overcame death, He didn't just overcome physical death. He overcame every kind of death there is. He took away death's power over us, by providing the certain promise of resurrection. And so we no longer need to fear death in any form. For wherever there is death, Jesus always provides a way to resurrection.

What is in danger of dying in your life just now? Happiness? Love? Confidence? Do not be afraid— death will not have the last word over you. You must begin now to pray for God to bring a resurrection.

DAY 161

*The righteous care
about justice for the poor,
but the wicked have no such concern.*
PROVERBS 29:7

JESUS constantly identified Himself with the poor. He lived with them, walked with them, and counted Himself as one of their number. How strange, then, that so many of Christ's followers today would never think of doing the same thing.

If the gospel is for anyone, it is for the poor. This has always been the case, though in the last century, the Western church has tried to make it into a gospel for the wealthy. The truth is that we are all paupers before God. But as long as you think you are rich, you will never accept that you need God. This is why the poor are typically more open to the good news of Christ, because they are not deluded with false notions of their own wealth.

Jesus identified Himself with the poor, the needy, and the outcasts more than with any other segment of society. If you wish to follow Christ sincerely, you must face this fact and decide how it will impact the way you live. Not if, but how. For you cannot expect to call yourself a follower of Christ if you are not willing to follow in His steps and do what He did.

That does not mean that you necessarily should take a vow of poverty—although God will certainly lead some to do this. What it does mean (for all of us) is that the needs of the poor should always be in the forefront of our thinking. The poor in body and the poor in spirit. The poor in third-world countries and the poor in your own community. You may not be wealthy, but you have far more than money to give. You have time, you have love, you have a listening ear, and you have strong hands.

"But I don't know anyone living in poverty." If that's true, it's not because the poor aren't right there—in your city, in your neighborhood. Find them. Spend time with them. When you do, you will find that Jesus is already there with them. He has been waiting to touch them through you—and you through them.

DAY 162

By wisdom a house is built,
and through understanding it is established;
through knowledge its rooms are filled
with rare and beautiful treasures.
PROVERBS 24:3–4

GOD'S wisdom is beautiful. And the man or woman who builds life upon God's wisdom will live a beautiful life. That is not to say that life will not be difficult, or that it will be free from sorrow. Wisdom never promises that. But it will be a beautiful life—full of rare treasures that only God's wisdom can bring.

What makes God's wisdom so beautiful? To start with, God's wisdom reflects God's heart and reveals His ways, and so it is beautiful for that reason. It brings a measure of peace and perspective to anyone who loves it, and so it is beautiful for that reason, as well. But perhaps the main reason God's wisdom is beautiful to the human heart is because it reveals something of the way life was supposed to be lived—before the Fall, before Adam and Eve set humanity on a course that took us away from God rather than toward Him. A life built on wisdom is built on the principles God intended life to follow. So there's something about a life of wisdom that is beautiful to us—because it looks something like the life of our dreams.

"But the wisdom that comes from heaven is first of all pure; then peace-loving, considerate, submissive, full of mercy and good fruit, impartial and sincere" (James 3:17). As a Christian, one of the best things you can do for yourself is to fall in love with God's wisdom. Because once you love His wisdom, you will pursue it—literally, you will hunt for it— with all your heart. And then what this verse proclaims will be true of the "house" that is your life.

DAY 163

Abram brought all these to him,
cut them in two and arranged the halves opposite
each other; the birds, however, he did not cut in half.
Then birds of prey came down on the carcasses,
but Abram drove them away.
GENESIS 15:10–11

WHENEVER we make any sort of sacrifice out of obedience to God, "birds of prey" will always come in and try to steal it away. Say, for example, you have decided to dedicate an hour each morning to prayer and Bible study. As soon as you begin to walk out this new commitment, you'll find your once-quiet mornings are suddenly filled with interruptions of all kinds. The phone will ring; people will come to the door; you'll suddenly begin sleeping through your alarm clock; your boss will ask you to come in earlier to the office. The "birds of prey" have arrived, right on schedule. . .to steal away your offering to God before you even have the chance to put it on the altar. Or let's say you decide to begin to tithe a full 10 percent of your income to your home church—as an expression of worship and dedication to God. Before you even write the check, the birds of prey begin to come: The car breaks down; a pipe in your basement springs a leak; and you discover you need to buy a new pair of glasses. Before you know it, your honest desire to sacrifice for God is stolen away.

Too many of our honest attempts at obedience are thwarted because we are caught unaware by Satan's schemes. He is a thief by nature, and he will always try to rob us of the very thing we have purposed to offer to God. We must learn to expect this and, like Abram, stand guard over our sacrifice to God. Don't allow circumstances to keep you from obedience.

*She gave this name
to the LORD who spoke to her:
"You are the God who sees me," for she said,
"I have now seen the One who sees me."*

GENESIS 16:13

BEFORE God showed up on the scene, Hagar was an outcast alone in the desert. And after He left, she was still in the same predicament. The thing that changed was not her circumstances but her understanding of God. She saw a quality in God, and she named it: "You are the God who sees me." That truth was enough to save her from despair and give her hope for a better future for her and her son.

Certain truths about God have the power to shield our hearts against despair, and those are the truths we must cling to the most tenaciously. One of these truths is the fact that God is good. Another is that God is all-powerful. And the third is that God sees you.

There will be times when you will speak to God, and He will not speak back. There will be times when you will cry out His name, and you will not find Him. But He is there, and He sees you. He sees your tears. He sees your heart. He sees your pain, your confusion, your anger, and your sorrow. He knows it all perfectly. And He is good—even though

He let this thing happen, even though He does not answer you right now. And He is all-powerful—even though His deliverance has not yet come, even though you are desperate for it.

"One thing God has spoken, two things have I heard: that you, O God, are strong, and that you, O LORD, are loving. . ." (Psalm 62:11–12). Like the psalmist, you will not despair as long as you hold onto these "shielding" truths. You may not understand everything God is doing; but there are certain things you know about Him. Cling to those truths— they will see you through the storm.

DAY 165

Joseph had a dream,
and when he told it to his brothers,
they hated him all the more.
GENESIS 37:5

WHEN God gives you a revelation, be very careful with whom you share it. Joseph's dream was from God—it was true, and Joseph knew it. And it even directly involved his family members. Nevertheless, for Joseph to go spouting it off to his brothers was a terribly bad idea—as he himself discovered after the fact. Joseph was certainly chosen of God. But that did not mean that he was necessarily wise. The same goes for you.

In fact, we are often unwise when it comes to dealing with a revelation from God. No sooner does God speak to us in a dream or a vision than we go running off to tell our friends. "I had a dream! I had a dream!" Perhaps we do it out of pride, or out of excitement, or just because we are naïve. But we often bring on ourselves an unnecessary load of grief.

Has God revealed something to you about your life? Your future? Your relationships? Then keep quiet about it, and let the thing stay between you and God. When or if God wants you to share the revelation, He will let you know. In the meantime, the best thing you can do is to believe what God has said—and shut up.

DAY 166

Then I said to you,
"Do not be terrified; do not be afraid of them.
The LORD your God, who is going before you,
will fight for you, as he did for you in Egypt,
before your very eyes, and in the desert.
There you saw how the LORD your God carried you,
as a father carries his son, all the way you went
until you reached this place." In spite of this,
you did not trust in the LORD your God, who went
ahead of you on your journey, in fire by night and in a
cloud by day, to search out places for you to camp and
to show you the way you should go. When the LORD
heard what you said, he was angry. . . .
DEUTERONOMY 1:29–34

THE more times we see God demonstrate His faithfulness in our lives, the more accountable we become to follow Him in faith the next time a challenge arises. The Lord was not angry with Israel simply because they failed to believe. They had not believed God in the beginning either—and He was not angry then. But He was angry now—because He had been revealing Himself to Israel for forty years, and when put to the test, they still did not believe.

If the Lord tests your faith when you are a young believer, it is no great danger if you fail. Such failure is an expected part of learning. But what if you are still failing the same test ten, twenty, forty years later? Then you may be in danger of wandering in deserts for the rest of your life.

The Lord is certainly patient with us, but He nevertheless expects us to mature in our faith. The Lord's patience and mercy are not excuses to keep acting like a toddler in the realms of spiritual growth. His kindness leads us to repentance and quiet trust, not to self-indulgent excuses.

Israel kept trying the patience of the Lord until at last He reached His limit. And, once the people crossed that line, the blessing of God was removed. The inheritance God had prepared for them was taken away. Is there some area of unbelief in your life that God has to keep addressing again and again?

It did not matter that the Israelites were camped right next to the Promised Land—so close that they could see it. Don't be lulled into thinking that keeping the truth in sight is the same thing as living it.

DAY 167

For the LORD your God is a consuming fire, a jealous God.
DEUTERONOMY 4:24

THE Lord is jealous to have the first place in our

love and affection—not for His own sake, but for ours. We desperately need to love Him above every possible competitor, because He is the pure source of all life and love and forgiveness and hope and everything good that we know. He knows this about Himself, and so He chooses to be jealous of our affections, because He loves us.

When God's love invades your life, it is like a fire, and it sets about consuming anything in your heart or circumstances that might be a competitor for God's affection. Things change when the fire of God's love hits, and not all of it is pleasant. You will, for example, suffer the loss of many things you love. You may lose habits, hobbies, friendships, possessions, ways of thinking of which you are particularly fond. The fire of God's jealousy burns them away, because He knows they threaten to steal your heart away from Him. And if that were to happen, your own heart would certainly die. Idolatry is a subtle sin; it can sometimes take hold before we even know it is there. And so out of love God consumes some things you have come to love.

When the fire of God's jealousy begins to consume some of the things you treasure, it's important that you understand why. Without understanding, God's behavior won't seem very loving at all, and you could easily fall into resentment and bitterness against Him. But once you understand the reason behind His jealousy, you realize that God's love is acting as a sentry over your soul. His love has claimed you as His own, and He is determined that nothing will ever be able to steal you away.

DAY 168

Joshua told the people,
"Consecrate yourselves, for tomorrow the LORD
will do amazing things among you."
JOSHUA 3:5

THERE are many times when God wants to do amazing things among us, but He does not, because we live as though we don't expect Him to do much of anything. We have not consecrated ourselves, which is to say we have done nothing to make room for God in our agendas. Of course, we'd love it if God would move in some miraculous manner, but we hardly expect such things from Him. "After all, He hasn't done anything in such a long time—at least not in my life." If this is how you think, then you have forgotten the awesomeness of God.

At its heart, consecration isn't about ritual or Old Testament law. It's about faith. When we consecrate ourselves, it's because we expect God to show up. We have faith that God can and will do amazing things in our lives. . .and so we prepare ourselves for

His imminent arrival. We get ready for a visitation from God.

When a guest comes to stay with you, you "consecrate" a room beforehand to prepare for her arrival. You clean the room; you put on fresh sheets; you open the windows and sweep the floor. And once the room is prepared, you keep it clean and available, so it will be ready the instant your guest arrives.

Spiritual consecration is a lot the same. We consecrate our hearts for God because we fully expect Him to arrive. His arrival may come today or tomorrow, but He will certainly come. And when He does, He will do amazing things among us.

DAY 169

Then Joshua said,
"You are witnesses against yourselves
that you have chosen to serve the LORD."
"Yes, we are witnesses," they replied.

JOSHUA 24:22

REMEMBER what you say to God on the mountain, because He will certainly put your words to the test as soon as you come down into the valley of everyday life. What did you say to God the last time you were caught up in worship? Did you promise to love Him? To obey Him in every small detail of life? To finally make that change in your attitude that His Spirit has been prodding you to make? Good—you have done well. But that is just the beginning of the process. We put our words to the test only in the valley. Why, then, are we so often surprised when the test comes—when God requires us to stand behind our words?

We all need a mountaintop encounter with God from time to time (but God is the only one who knows when we need such an experience). While we are on the mountain with God, we see with clarity. We understand. From that place, we catch some glimpse of God's great love. Such encounters with God are real. They are life.

But they are not everyday life. Everyday life is real, too. But it's grittier. It's not as clear—in fact it's downright muddy at times. And it's the place where everything we said to God on the mountain is tested. Purified. Made real.

You see, the words of devotion and commitment and love that we spill out to God in moments of spiritual fervor aren't real until they're tested. That is, they aren't real until they've stood the test and been proven true. Your commitment isn't true until you live it, until it becomes a part of you.

The mountain is where it begins. But real, abundant life only comes to maturity in the valley.

DAY 170

"If serving the LORD seems undesirable to you,
then choose for yourselves this day whom you will serve,
whether the gods your forefathers served beyond
the River, or the gods of the Amorites,
in whose land you are living. But as for me
and my household, we will serve the LORD."

JOSHUA 24:15

THE decision to serve God must be made every morning upon awakening, because if you don't make it then, you will inevitably turn to serve the first distraction that presents itself.

"Oh, the kitchen is a mess—I should clean it up."

"I really should check my E-mail before I do anything else."

"My kids won't give me a moment's peace!"

"I just can't seem to find time to do the things God wants me to do," we end up saying. These days, everyone is busy. But for a Christian walking with God, there should always be enough time in the day to do everything life requires—especially those things God has commanded.

If your life is too busy for you to obey God, what is stealing your time from Him? Phone calls? Fun diversions? Everyday errands? Your life may be full of such distractions—most everyone's life is—but it is up to you whether you let them rule you. Beware of filling your life with too many things, or else you will find yourself trapped in a pattern of constantly "reacting" to one thing or another throughout the day. That is not a Spirit-led life, but a life ruled by circumstances. The Holy Spirit knows that life is full of distractions, and He is perfectly capable of leading you to deal with each of them in due course.

DAY 171

When the angel of the LORD appeared to Gideon, he said, "The LORD is with you, mighty warrior." "But sir," Gideon replied, "if the LORD is with us, why has all this happened to us? Where are all his wonders that our fathers told us about when they said, 'Did not the LORD bring us up out of Egypt?' But now the LORD has abandoned us and put us into the hand of Midian." The LORD turned to him and said, "Go in the strength you have and save Israel out of Midian's hand. Am I not sending you?" But Lord," Gideon asked, "how can I save Israel? My clan is the weakest in Manasseh, and I am the least in my family." The LORD answered, "I will be with you, and you will strike down all the Midianites together."

JUDGES 6:12–16

BEFORE God came to him, Gideon's view of life was too narrow and far too limiting. He evaluated everything—including his own potential—from a purely human perspective. The presence, power, and purposes of God never figured into his calculations. No doubt he believed God existed. But he no longer believed that God was near. "But now the Lord has abandoned us and put us into the hand of Midian."

Consequently, Gideon fled from his enemies. He hid in a cellar and set about the business of surviving—because that was the best someone of his ability could hope for. It probably never once occurred to him to try for victory. That would have made no practical sense at all, since he was so very small and so very limited in strength. At least, that was what he believed.

The fact is that Gideon's assessment of himself was wrong, because it ignored the reality of God's presence in his life. Gideon's evaluation of things was not made in the context of faith, and that effectively blinded him from seeing all the resources at his disposal.

Oftentimes we make the same mistake Gideon did. Beware of evaluating yourself in purely human terms; always keep God's perspective in mind. When God came to Gideon, the first thing He said was, "The Lord is with you, mighty warrior." God did not name Gideon for who he was in human terms, but for who he would be in God's hands.

Since we live by the Spirit,
let us keep in step with the Spirit.
GALATIANS 5:25

LONG before we can hope to follow God boldly in the external choices of our daily lives, we must learn to follow God in our inner lives, that is, in our thoughts and feelings. The Spirit's leading within us must overrule all the other competing voices, so that we follow His will even when it goes against all human voices of logic, desire, need, and emotion. That is not to say that God is not logical, He is the Father of logic, after all, or that He does not care deeply about our feelings, our needs, and desires. But God's Spirit has an advantage of perspective that we can never match. He sees the long view, which sometimes means His Spirit will lead in a direction that, from our short-view human perspective, seems illogical or even blind to our needs in the here and now.

Too often, though, we exalt reason or emotion so highly that God's Spirit doesn't have a chance to get through to us. "That can't be God; it doesn't seem logical to me." Or "I think this is what God wants for me because it feels so right." How often do we deny God's Spirit when His leading doesn't sound reasonable to us, or when it doesn't match up with our feelings? You should, of course, apply your reason to every situation you face. And you should respect your feelings. But you should never make either one of them idols. Never use your human reason or your emotions as an excuse not to trust God extravagantly.

DAY 173

After six days Jesus took Peter,
James and John with him and led them up a high
mountain, where they were all alone.
There he was transfigured before them.
MARK 9:2

THERE will be times in your walk with Christ when He will want to lead you away from everyone and get you by Himself. When you begin to feel the Spirit pull you toward solitude, you must immediately drop everything and go. Don't ignore it. Don't put it off for a more convenient time. Don't make excuses. Just go. The Lord has a reason for calling you away—there are things He wants to tell you, show you, share with you—and it would be the height of foolishness not to heed His call.

Jesus simply will not share some things with you in a crowd. What secrets has Jesus shared with you lately—just between the two of you? What treasures has He brought to you in your private times together?

What do you know about Christ that you learned directly from Him—not through a pastor or the latest Christian book?

We need our corporate times of revelation, of course. Together we are the body of Christ. I can't know Him fully apart from you, nor you from me. But we also need times of private revelation and communion with Him. Without those private times, Jesus gradually becomes someone we experience, but do not really know. To know Him, we must let Him lead us away from our crowded lives to lonely high places where we can speak one on one. There are things He wants to tell you, treasures He wants you to have. But first He has to get you completely to Himself.

DAY 174

"Do not be afraid,
O man highly esteemed," he said. "Peace!
Be strong now; be strong." When he spoke to me,
I was strengthened and said, "Speak, my lord,
since you have given me strength."

DANIEL 10:19

THERE is a rawness that comes from being in the presence of God. There is a stripping of every pretense, every lie, every ounce of false bravado we have projected on the world or into our own minds.

There is a nakedness of soul. An absolute helplessness. We are, quite simply, undone by God's presence. By seeing Him, we see ourselves and recognize that we are nothing by comparison. And we are filled with remorse that we could have ever thought otherwise.

The presence of God inspires fear, not because He is malicious but because He is so much more grand and more powerful and more holy than we ever could have imagined. But the presence of God also inspires hope, because in the midst of all of His holiness, He does not destroy us. We are not consumed. Instead, He extends to us His hand and says, "Do not be afraid! . . . Be strong now; be strong." And then this miracle occurs within us. God's speaking gives us strength, changes us. We are not the same people we were just a moment ago.

Never run from the rawness of God's presence, for it is the only place where we can ultimately be convinced that we are completely accepted in the beloved.

DAY 175

*In those days Israel had no king;
everyone did as he saw fit.*
JUDGES 21:25

THE Book of Judges tells the story of what happens when people try to make God a god of convenience.

Israel did not need a human king—a fact that Samuel later made abundantly clear. They needed to submit to the King they already had. But that was not convenient, and so they were not willing. Instead they tried to fit Him in as circumstances allowed, and when things got really rough, they ran to Him for rescue.

Our God is many things—holy, loving, forgiving, powerful, compassionate, and wise. But He is not convenient. If you follow Him, He will inevitably blow away all the plans you laid for how life should go. It isn't your life anymore—it's His. And His plan, though different from yours, is always better—always. Without exception.

And, of course, we know this. It's amazing, then, how often we still buck against the inconvenience of it all. . .

"I know I shouldn't sleep with my boyfriend, but we are so much in love, after all. I think God must understand that."

"Maybe I shouldn't have seen that movie, but everyone was raving about it so much, I just couldn't resist."

"Sure, I would like to do more for the poor, but my schedule is just so full as it is. I know God wouldn't want me to run myself ragged."

Treating God's lordship as a matter of convenience will always lead us to a life that mixes the holy and the profane. It is a life without power or joy or any clear purpose. It is a life without God. God is not a god of convenience.

DAY 176

"Do not keep talking so proudly
or let your mouth speak such
arrogance, for the LORD is a God who knows,
and by him deeds are weighed."

1 SAMUEL 2:3

THE truths Hannah wrote in this verse she learned during her barrenness. Or perhaps you could say she learned them from her barrenness, for it was her barrenness that drove her to God in the first place. Her barrenness pressed her to seek God in "hope against hope," and her barrenness eventually opened her eyes so that she could see that whether God opened her womb or not, "the Lord is a God who knows."

Of course, there are many kinds of barrenness. Chances are you struggle with some sort of barrenness in your soul, some empty place within you that has remained unfilled for as long as you can remember, so long that you genuinely wonder whether you might be flawed in some way, that your empty place has an irreparable leak, one that will prevent the emptiness from ever being filled. Not many know about your barrenness, of course. Perhaps no one knows. You are careful to keep it hidden from public view lest you get ridiculed or judged by those who don't share the same struggle (which is precisely what happened to Hannah, if you'll recall).

We are all barren, you see. It is by the mercy of God that He provokes some of us to recognize that fact. God may one day lead us into a fertile place of fulfillment and joy—but in the meantime, He comes to us because of our barrenness, in the midst of it.

DAY 177

*The boy Samuel
ministered before the LORD under Eli.
In those days the word of the LORD was rare;
there were not many visions.*

1 SAMUEL 3:1

THERE are seasons in every Christian's life when God is inexplicably silent. In your outward circumstances, nothing has changed. You are still walking the same line of obedience to God that you were before, but then the visions suddenly stop. The voice of the Holy Spirit, which you had enjoyed on a daily basis, goes mute. And the Word of God becomes horribly dry, sounding to your soul more like a textbook than any sort of living text.

Are you in sin? Is God displeased with you somehow? Are you missing God's will for your life? Perhaps; but maybe not. The Holy Spirit moves in ways that are mysterious. We cannot easily explain them, but we can learn to be at peace with them.

Jesus told us that those who are born of the Spirit will always experience this sense of mystery in following God. "The wind blows wherever it pleases. You hear its sound, but you cannot tell where it comes from or where it is going. So it is with everyone born of the Spirit" (John 3:8). Sometimes the wind is still. And there is nothing wrong with that.

"But how can I follow God if He is silent? What should I do?" God is never completely silent, of course, since we have the Word. What does the Word say to do? Start there. And when God was speaking to you, what did He tell you to do? Did you obey? Fully? Then perhaps you can start there, as well.

When God needs to speak to you, He will. Until then, be obedient to the Truth. And learn what it means to commune with the God of silence.

DAY 178

Then the LORD called Samuel.
Samuel answered, "Here I am."
And he ran to Eli and said, "Here I am;
you called me." But Eli said, "I did not call;
go back and lie down." So he went and lay down.
1 SAMUEL 3:4–5

TOO often we mistake the voice of God for the voice of organized religion, or vice versa. And although some believe the two are supposed to be the same thing, most times they are not. We make two mistakes along these lines: Like Samuel, we hear the call of God in our hearts, and we immediately run to the organized church to tell us what God is saying. Or else the leaders of our religion issue a call to us, and we immediately assume the call is from God.

When you sense the call of God in your heart, don't go to organized religion and ask, "What do you want me to do?" Organized religion didn't call you; God did. God is the One who appoints some to be apostles, some prophets, some teachers and evangelists. And when religious leaders actually try to play God in this way (which, sadly, many of them do), they generally miss the mark—often by a considerable margin.

So when God calls you, be quiet about it until God brings clarity to the calling He's placed on you. The role of the church—the body of Christ—is to keep you from error by teaching you how to walk with God, so that you can hear Him and obey His call. In the same way, Eli could try to teach Samuel, but ultimately, Eli had no idea what God was calling Samuel to be. That was between Samuel and the Spirit of God.

The same is true for you.

*The LORD your God will drive out
those nations before you, little by little.
You will not be allowed to eliminate them all at once,
or the wild animals will multiply around you.*
DEUTERONOMY 7:22

GOD has chosen gladly to give you His kingdom. But He will not allow you to possess it quickly. God has set up the spiritual life so that entering the Promised Land of abundant life in Christ takes time. A lot of time. And it does not come without a fight.

On the surface, this sounds contradictory. If God is so thrilled about giving me the kingdom, why does He make it so hard for me to actually get it? For the same reason that He didn't allow the people of Israel to possess the Promised Land overnight. It was too big for them to handle all at once. They needed to grow into it. And so do we. Although this fact of spiritual growth can be frustrating, in a way it's actually very good news—because it means that we really have no idea how big and awesome our inheritance in Christ actually is.

Trust the pace God has set for you in your spiritual growth. He knows what you can handle by way of trials or blessings. He has chosen gladly to give you the Kingdom, but at a pace that is exactly right for you. For instance, you may need to learn more about the kingdom by being single; one day God may also

call you to build His kingdom through being married
Either way, trust Him. He knows what He's doing.

DAY 180

Neither before nor after Josiah was there a king like him who turned to the LORD as he did—with all his heart and with all his soul and with all his strength, in accordance with all the Law of Moses.
2 KINGS 23:25

WHAT made Josiah different? These two things: He listened to the truth, and he thought for himself. These two qualities are essential for anyone who wants to be extraordinary in God.

The sad part of Josiah's story is that it is so uncommon, both among the kings of Israel and Judah and among believers in the present age. How can a man or woman have the living God come to live within them and the result not be extraordinary? And yet so many Christians manage to live very small, run-of-the-mill lives. They do not see how beautiful they are in Christ—how overwhelmingly loved. . .how rich with potential and purpose and power.

Do you see how beautiful you are in Christ?

The fact of the matter is that we are all extraordinary in God. But only a few have the faith to see it, and even fewer are brazen enough to act as though it is true.

Inspirational Library